Not Enough

By Ada Brooks

Hidden Shelf Publishing House
P.O. Box 4168, McCall, ID 83638
www.hiddenshelfpublishinghouse.com

Not Enough

Artist: Megan Whitfield (Cover, Pg. 133),
Ada Brooks (Pg. 130)

Editor: Robert D. Gaines

Graphic design: Allison Kaukola

Interior layout: Kerstin Stokes

Publisher's Cataloging-in-Publication Data

Names: Brooks, Ada, author.
Title: Not enough / Ada Brooks.
Description: McCall, ID: Hidden Shelf Publishing House, 2023.
Identifiers: ISBN: 978-1-955893-17-6 (paperback) | 978-1-955893-21-3 (ebook) | 978-1-955893-22-0 (epub) Subjects: LCSH Brooks, Ada. | Teenagers--Biography. | Teenage girls--Biography. | Anxiety--Patients--United States--Biography. | Man-woman relationships--Biography. | Dating violence. | Victims of dating violence--United States. | Teenage girls--Abuse of--United States. | BISAC BIOGRAPHY & AUTOBIOGRAPHY / Women Classification: LCC HQ798 .B76 2023 | DDC 305.235/2/092--dc2

Table of Contents

Chapter 1
Smoke-Stained Existence

With my back against the wall and knees pulled up as far as my breasts allow, I sit in silence, plagued with fear. Using the end of one cigarette to light the next, I'm smoking like a criminal sentenced to the gallows. I tap my ash into the green plastic tray overflowing with cigarette butts and roaches smoked earlier that week. My anxiety is choking me like a noose. I'm waiting for results I already know.

I force myself to look at the bruising on my wrist. Slowly removing the bandage, I see the swelling has lessened over the last several days. The bruising was purplish-blue at first. Now it's morphing into a putrid green, like a newborn's dirty diaper, muddied with yellow splotches. A tear rolls down my face. I rewrap my wrist, take a deep breath, cough, and light another cigarette.

Scanning Devin's room, taking visual snapshots of the tiny world I've become accustomed to, I realize that I am in my own personal prison. The walls are paneled with sheets of fake wood and smoke-stained blinds cover a lone window overlooking the neighbor's newly shingled rooftop. One small closet and an unusually large bathroom sum up the structural characteristics of my cell.

Devin's bed is a single mattress and box spring on the floor. It's draped with navy blue sheets, a few worn pillows, and an itchy polyester bedspread. An old coffee table under the window on the far wall serves as a makeshift entertainment stand. On it is a covered record player, a small modern cassette player, and a thirteen-inch television with a built-in VCR. Scented candles and incense burners are scattered on every flat surface of this mismatched, retro-modern system.

Music and movie posters cover nearly all the brown panels in the room. The one I want to rip down is not the picture of a malnourished redhead with big bosoms. Rather, it's a poster from the Stanley Kubrick movie, *A Clockwork Orange*. You've surely seen it. Malcolm McDowell plays the leader of a sadistic gang that takes pleasure in raping and robbing during the midnight hours. This poster features his piercing blue eyes that scrutinize me daily and penetrate through my stomach like a serrated knife.

If I'm not with Devin—or at school, work, or home—he assumes I am running around with my best friend, Gabby, walking the streets and fucking or sucking off any random guy who flashes us a wink or a smile. When I am with Gabby, we are normally in her bedroom smoking and playing cards or video games. Devin's bullshit allegations are hurtful and flat-out ridiculous.

His jealousy began when we started dating. I thought it was cute at first and it made me feel like he really wanted to be with me. But now, Devin's behavior is spiraling out of control and I don't know why or what to do about it. I stay with him because I love him. Don't get me wrong, I know it's not right and I know I don't deserve the emotional scars.

I am more nervous than ever. My hands are shaking uncontrollably. Devin went to the gas station for more cigarettes. It's right around the corner and I don't know what's taking so long. It may have only been a few minutes since he left, but it feels like an eternity. My nerves are exploding!

Because of Devin's volatile reaction to the mere suggestion of me being pregnant, it's hard to predict the severity of this evening. I'm preparing for the worst.

Chapter 2
Candy Bars and Condoms

I 'm in the spring semester of my senior year; Grand Landing High School, Class of 1992. Being an upperclassman with a high GPA but no burning desire to take college prep classes, I opted out of the full school day and entered the work-study program. Perfect for someone who loathes school, it frees me up to leave after fourth period.

With the help of my Marketing teacher, Mrs. Hansen, I landed a job as a cashier at Med Warehouse, a discount drug store on the east side of town.

As a Med Warehouse cashier, it's impossible not to notice the merchandise customers toss on the conveyor belt during check out. A lot of locals shop here. Old Mr. Creeks buys a large tube of hemorrhoid cream every Sunday. Mark Small, who works at the Radio Shack next door, buys "Ribbed for Her Pleasure" condoms and extra-strength jock itch cream at least once a week. My first day on the job, Mrs. Meyers, an English teacher at Grand Landing, bought a National Inquirer, five king-sized Hershey bars, a bottle of weight loss pills, and a three-pack box of enemas.

Always pleasant to the customers, I greet them with bright eyes and a chipper smile. "Hello, how are you today? Did you find everything you were looking for?"

At work, I make a conscious effort to be sensitive to what others are likely to view as their personal shortcomings. Embarrassment and humiliation are two emotions I'd rather not experience myself, so I never call attention to the severe acne face scrub or lice exterminating shampoos. I ring these products up as if they are nail clippers and cotton balls.

The storefront is mostly panels of glass that frame the sky. This evening, it's glowing with warm hues of orange and red. Some yellow sneaks into the palette and makes it look even more majestic against the dark blue. It's a stunning watercolor painted on the sky but vanishes into the darkness in a matter of minutes.

It's Friday night and approaching nine o'clock. The store is closing soon and my shift is almost over. After ringing up the third pregnancy test of the night, it occurs to me that I am almost two weeks late. Between customers, I straighten the merchandise on the impulse-buy rack. I can't stop thinking about the possibility of being pregnant. It terrifies me and excites me at the same time!

My thoughts come to a sudden halt when Penny's voice booms over the intercom that's set to a volume so loud shoppers cover their ears. Penny, the night manager, begins reading the announcement for the store closing. Stragglers make their final selections and begin to line up at the checkout lanes.

I dash over to Customer Service where Penny is counting out her cash drawer. My sudden appearance makes her jump like a spider cricket in the bathtub when you turn on the light. Her hand is full of nickels, and they fly up and onto the linoleum floor.

"Oh no, I'm sorry, Penny," I say as I crouch down and start picking up the change.

"That's alright, sweetheart, what's up? You scared the bah-Jesus outta me!"

Penny's the cool manager at Med Warehouse. She always treats us teenage employees with respect, not like blundering idiot children with no common sense and a dead-end future. Dan Munky, the assistant night manager acts like that. Once, he asked me if I used the toilet before my shift because "it will be a while before my lunch break." I still can't believe he asked me that! I'm not five years old and going on a family road trip. *Holy crap, what an ass!*

I catch Penny's attention. "Before you cash out all the drawers, Penny, will you please do me a favor and ring me up? I'm not working this weekend and there are a few things I need to buy before we close tonight."

"Of course, darlin'... no-pro-blem-o. Let's see, how 'bout I close down your register first? That way you can gather up what you're fixin' to buy, and I'll take care of ya at Misty's register. How's that sound to ya, buttercup?"

I glance at my checkout line to see if anyone is

waiting. "Sounds great, you're the best!"

Walking back to my register, my heart is beating like it's competing in the 100-yard-dash. *Relax, Rose, relax!* I try all the techniques I know. I breathe in through my nose and out through my mouth slowly, tighten my ass and squeeze my fists to release nervous energy, and count backward from fifty to one. Nothing helps.

"You betcha' chick-a pea." I hear Penny say in the distance as I walk back to my register.

A lot of employees and customers of Med Warehouse are annoyed by Penny's sweet vernacular. I'm pretty sure she never gets through a sentence without saying darlin', sweetheart, hon', sugar pie, or baby. I find it as endearing as her small, sweet stature and strong Southern accent. She moved here from Georgia a few years ago. I don't know the purpose of her demographic shift, but I'm glad she's here.

Penny embodies the stereotypical "southern hospitality." She reminds me of Dolly Parton's portrayal of the patient, sweet, and loving southern beauty in my mom's favorite movie, *Steel Magnolias*. I'll never understand why it's her favorite because it always makes her cry. Anyhow, Penny exudes a genuineness and tender warmth that makes me want to be special to her.

After ringing up a bottle of night-time cold medicine, a carton of Salem Light cigarettes, a couple bottles of fruit-flavored antacid tablets, and a muscle car magazine, Penny signals me with her eyes to turn off my register light. Excited to do my own shopping, I politely tell a young mother with a toddler on her hip and baby rash ointment in her hand that she can check out at register four.

Speed walking to the back room, I crash full force into the swinging door. *I hope nobody saw that.* I clock out for the night. First stop, the feminine hygiene aisle. I make a quick comparison of prices and aesthetic appeal and grab an e.p.t test off the shelf. To seem not so eager, I also pick up deodorant, shampoo, a Milky Way for Mom, and a Kit-Kat for Devin. I need a pack of Marlboro Lights but won't buy them here. Rational or not, I don't want Penny to know I smoke. I fear she'll think less of me.

"Are you ready, sweet one?" Penny asks as I round the greeting cards aisle to where she is waiting for me at Misty's register.

I'm glad to see Misty has left for the night. Penny and I, the custodial staff, and the head janitor, who doubles as our security officer, are the only people in the store. I put my stuff on the conveyor belt and take out my wallet. Penny scans each item, enters my employee discount code, and tells me the total, seventeen dollars and fifty-three cents. Not a word is spoken about the pregnancy test. *Penny's discretion is appreciated.*

"Thanks, Penny." I pick up my shopping bag and stuff it into my oversized denim purse. I walk quickly to the exit door and say, "Have a great weekend!"

"You too sugar dumplin' ... see you next week."

***

Not Enough

Misty, my teenage co-worker, and I seldom interact. I see her as being an attractive girl whose personality and people skills are sadly unexceptional. I think my negativity toward her started when it became blatantly obvious that Misty thinks of herself as being on a higher level than others, and therefore should be respected by everyone who's not her. She rarely smiles and barely speaks to anyone who checks out at her lane. Using the store's old and dusty register, she is careful not to chip her finely shaped acrylic fingernails. Every time we work together, I notice they are painted with precision to match her array of stylish outfits, shoes, and handbags.

Misty's demeanor, while working with us middle-class mortals, reeks of resentment. I assume her uppity attitude derives from her comfortable lifestyle in Pine's Manor, an exclusive gated neighborhood. Her father is a successful defense lawyer, and her mother is the queen of the town's socialites and throws charity galas for homeless kids.

On the flip side, my mom and I live in the Parkview Terrace Townhomes. I was told that these homes used to be in high demand because of the beautiful view of Town Park. The park had once been filled with blossoming dogwood trees and flowers that filled the air with scents of lilies, and honeysuckle. It had wooden benches circling around a small pond where ducks flourished. A water fountain of a baby cherub put out streams of water from its puckered lips down to the birdbath below. Families would have cookouts, picnics, reunions, and other mushy movie scene gatherings.

Over the years, as the neighborhood declined and people moved away, Town Park fell into disrepair. Now, it's a gathering place for dropouts and folks down on their luck. Local drunkards hide their faces from the sun with old newspapers and kids play kick the can with the empty beer cans strewn about. Those children have no idea that their dirt-trodden playground was once a bower of flowering blossoms, laughter, and happiness.

***

With a hundred fluorescent tubes lighting the Med Warehouse's interior, I have to wait a few seconds for my eyes to adjust to the clear black sky. Making my way across the dimly lit parking lot, I carry pepper spray in hand. I look left and right for possible predators. I see nothing but a stray cat eating French fries. I look under my car to see if anyone is there waiting to slash my ankles and drag me away to an uncertain but most definitely bloody and painful death. I see no one. Sliding into my blue Honda Civic, I take the shopping bag out of my purse and toss it onto the passenger seat. I lock the doors and turn the key. I sit for a minute, letting the old girl warm up. Meanwhile, I turn on the radio and sing along with Cyndi Lauper to *Girls Just Wanna Have Fun*. I fasten my seat belt, turn on the headlights, and check the mirrors. I release the parking brake, engage the clutch, shift into first gear and leave the solitude of the parking lot to go see Devin.

Chapter 3

A Dirty Boy's Bedroom

*I*t's a quarter to ten when I get to Devin's neighborhood and make my final turn onto Gulliver Way. In the two-story gray house on the hill, Devin lives with his parents and little brother, Nate. I pull into the driveway and catch a glimpse of two little eyes peeking out from behind the curtains. I grab my purse and my Med Warehouse bag with the e.p.t. box and get out of the car.

Welcomed by the "Our House is Neat—Wipe your Feet" doormat, I dutifully wipe my shoes and ring the doorbell. Nate opens the door no more than a half-second after my finger touches the bell.

"Hey, little man, what's happenin'?" I hold my hand up for a high-five hello.

"Rose, um, right now, your car's like, um, rolling down the driveway."

"What? Oh my God!" I turn around quickly to run after my car and whack Nate square in his face with my bag.

I was so lost in thought when I got here, I forgot to pull the emergency brake! Running alongside the car, I open the door and dive in head-first. I yank the brake up and my car comes to a stumbling stop. Short of breath from the excitement, I lie on the front seat with my legs and backside hanging out. I look as stupid as I feel.

Relieved to see my car didn't take out any neighborhood pets, I get in and move it from the middle of the street and back up onto the driveway. Pressing the clutch, I shift into first gear, pull hard on the emergency brake, and shut off the ignition. *Shit, that was crazy!* Disheveled, I tug on my clothes, and once again, walk to the front door.

"So, Nate, how about that Looney Tune production? Pretty exciting, huh?"

"Um, yeah, that was like, nuts," he replies, looking up at me with his colossal green eyes.

"I'm sorry I hit you with my bag, Nate. Are you okay?"

"Yeah, I'm okay. Are you?"

Nate, bless his heart, is really thoughtful for a little kid. He didn't scream out or laugh as most other five-year-olds would. Even at his young age, I consider him an old soul, sensitive and wise beyond his years.

Mr. and Mrs. Miller waited until Devin was fourteen before having another child. I don't know If Nate's conception was planned, a happy accident, or a mid-life crisis. Fourteen years seems like an odd length between siblings. *But then, what do I know?* Whatever the reason, Nate is an irreplaceable piece in The Miller's

Family puzzle.

"You're so sweet, Nate, I could just take a big ol' bite out of you." I also want to squeeze his plump little cheeks, but resist. I never met a kid who enjoyed the humility of having their face pinched. "Is Devin home?"

"Yep, he's in his room." Nate turns toward the staircase. "Deeev- innn, your whoa-man's here," he hollers.

As Nate skips back to the living room to watch *The Mighty Ducks* with his parents, I chuckle and head upstairs to Devin's room.

Devin meets me at his bedroom door. "Hey, Rose, didn't think I was gonna see you tonight."

"Well, surprise, here I am. I hope that's okay with you." *Geez!*

"Of course, it is, babe. I said I didn't expect to see you, not that I didn't want to see you. Come in, sit down … take off your clothes." Devin smirks as he rubs his stomach under his shirt. I stand on my toes and kiss him. I taste resin on his lips. He reaches his long arms around me and gives my butt a tight squeeze, then pats it lightly while guiding me into his room.

Devin's not a brawny guy. He's 6'4" and thin, but very strong. His black wavy hair frames his face, a face as close to perfection as I've ever seen. With his ocean blue eyes, a triangular nose, strong jaw line, and a beautiful mouth beckoning to be kissed, he is strikingly handsome. *He captivates me!*

As Devin closes the door behind us, I hear the soft click of the lock. The lights are off. Candlelight and contrasting colors on the TV screen obscurely illuminate the room. The scent of incense is heavy. The window is open about two inches and a small red desk fan balances on the windowsill, drawing the stench of marijuana and black cherry out of the room.

Devin is high, but he packs the bowl again. "You wanna hit?"

"Nah, not right now. You go ahead if you want." Surprised, he looks at me and says, "I packed it for you. Turning down the first hit, Rose? That's not like you. You always want to break green. What's wrong with you?"

"Nothing." Needing to push this conversation my way, I add, "I've been thinking about you a lot today." I glance over where my purse and shopping bag are on the floor.

"Oh yeah? Does that mean we're gonna get naked soon? My pants are starting to bulge just looking at you." He shifts his eyebrows up and down.

Keeping my voice sweet, not bitter, I say, "Devin, get your mind out of my pants for one minute, please. I really need to talk to you."

His face turns from playful to pissed off. He notices the Med Warehouse bag. "What's that?"

"Well, actually, it's kind of what I want to talk to you about." I reach for the bag and put it on my lap. "I got you a Kit-Kat bar." With a stupid grin on my face, I take the candy out and hand it to him.

My next move is to strategically and gently ease him into the baby conversation. While I dig through the bag, Devin is looking over my shoulder and spots the e.p.t. box.

"What the hell?" He's angry. "You better have picked that up for your slutty ass friend, Gabby!" *Great, I can see how this is gonna play out.*

My anxiety kicks into full gear and I start to tremble nervously. I light a cigarette from his pack. He smokes menthols, Newport 100's ... not my brand, but they'll make do.

"No, Devin, actually, it's for me. I'm almost two weeks late."

"Jesus Christ, Rose! Are you fucking kidding me? I thought you were on the pill!"

"I am on the pill, Devin!"

"Then how the hell can you be pregnant?"

I hang my head, feeling like my heart's been ripped out and stomped on the ground. He may as well have spit on me.

"It works ninety-eight percent of the time," I reply in a whisper.

"Oh, I see. And you're so special, so unique that a birth control pill works for pretty much every woman in the whole fucking world, but not for you. I swear to God, Rose, you live in a fucking fairy tale. I don't need this shit. Not now!"

My chest tightens, and a sharp pain jabs my ribcage.

"Besides," he spews, "how can I even be certain it's mine? Oh, I know, we can go on the Maury Povich show and take one of those 'Who's your Baby's Daddy' lie detector tests. Doesn't that sound fun, Rose? You can prove to me and everyone else in the world that you really are a little whore!"

Ready, set, and the bashing begins.

Chapter 4
Exit Denied

*I*t's the tenth time tonight he calls me a whore. Something in me ignites. I stand up, take a deep breath, and let loose.

"This is total bullshit, Devin! When I'm not with you in this cellblock of a bedroom, I'm home with my mom, at school, at work, or at Gabby's house! Not having group sex! I'm sick of this shit! No, I'm sick of you and your overactive jealous imagination! You know what? I don't even care! Fuck you! I'm not taking this anymore! I hate you! I am so fucking outta here."

"You're not going anywhere," Devin screeches.

This is the first time I stand up to him and judging from his furrowed brow he's baffled by it. Unwilling to pause and reflect on my feelings, his confusion turns into anger. I fear I made it worse.

He stands feet spread in front of the bedroom door blocking my escape.

"Get out of my way," I yell. He doesn't budge. Using every ounce of strength I have, I somehow channel my fear into anger. Determined to leave, I push him as hard as I can. He doesn't move. *Damn it!*

"Give it up, Rose," he laughs. "You're making an ass out of yourself."

I give him another push.

"Rose, I said give it up. You're not going anywhere. We need to talk!"

Oh my God, now he wants to talk? Are you fucking kidding me?

My eyes are burning, my body is exhausted. *When is this going to stop?*

I notice Devin ease his stance a bit. I reach around him and grab the brass doorknob. He clenches my wrist with both hands and twists it off the knob. He jerks me back and forth, bangs my head on the wall, then throws me onto his bed.

Sobbing, I curl up my body and rock back and forth. The blanket soaks up my tears and I become keenly aware of the throbbing in my head and wrist. What do I do now? Why did he do that? I'm stunned. Whipping me with hateful words is bad enough. Physical abuse? He's never done that before. *Oh, dear Lord, please help me!*

After pacing for a few minutes, Devin sits down beside me and runs his long fingers through my hair. He leans over and kisses me on top of my head. I want to punch him in the face, mess up that pretty nose of his. "I'm sorry Rose. I didn't mean to hurt you, I love you, please forgive me." He pauses to gauge my reaction. I don't have one. "Please don't leave me,

21

Rose. I need you, baby, you mean the world to me. I'm just a little freaked out right now, okay? I need time to let this sink in. Okay? I know I'm not thinking clearly and I'm sorry."

With choppy breath, I stammer, "I don't even know if I'm pregnant yet or not. I'm a little freaked out too, you know." I cough from crying so hard and cover my face with both of my hands. "I expected a different reaction from you, Devin. I swear, I thought you'd be happy."

"I'm sorry baby, I love you so much and I know I overreact sometimes. I know you stay true to me. I just say those things because I'm scared of losing you." I've heard that explanation more than once but will never understand why he thinks saying hateful things will improve a situation or encourage anyone to stick around. *Makes no fucking sense!*

"Let's just wait a week," he continues, "and if you still haven't started, then you can do the test. Okay? I love you, Rose. You know that, don't you?" Reaching over, he wraps his hands around mine, uncovering my face. He wipes away a tear with his thumb. "Come on and give me a hug. You're so beautiful. I hate it when I make you cry."

I push his hands away and wipe my nose with my sleeve. Standing up, I look straight in his eyes and deny him his hug and apology. Saying nothing, I walk into the bathroom. I stare at the mirror. Black mascara is running down my face. My hair is a tangled blonde mess. My eyes are red and puffy. I look like a pug with an eye infection. *Yeah, right, I'm so beautiful.* Worse than feeling like I've been beaten with the nastiest of ugly sticks, my throbbing head is killing me and my bruised wrist is swelling. It hurts like hell!

Devin walks into the bathroom, stands behind me, and puts his hands on my shoulders. I reluctantly turn around, and he looks down at my injured wrist.

"I think I need some ice for it," I say, keeping my eyes grounded on the floor.

"Okay, baby," he says sweetly. "I'll go get you some ice."

Before stepping out of the bathroom, I take another look in the mirror. I'm sickened by the sight of my reflection. Right now, I don't care if I am pregnant or not. I pick up the pipe Devin packed earlier and hit it again and again. Caution be damned! With each inhale I pray for escape. If Devin refuses to let me leave physically, I'm going to do my best to be mentally absent. *Where's a pair of those fucking ruby slippers when I need them?*

Devin comes back to his bedroom with a bag of frozen peas, a glass of Pepsi with crushed ice, just the way I like it, and a bottle of Tylenol. I take a couple of pills and wash them down with the Pepsi, balance the frozen vegetables on my wrist, and continue to hit the bowl.

Neither of us speaks for a long time. He puts two cigarettes in his mouth, lights them both, and hands me one. The menthol tastes different after I smoke weed. It's like eating a peppermint patty after drinking lemonade. I stub the cigarette out and lie back on the bed.

"Yuck," I say under my breath.

"What, Rose? Did you say something?" Devin asks.

Mumbling, I respond, "I said, we'll wait and if I don't start then I'll take the test."

He kisses me on top of my head. "Okay, baby."

Still holding on to the frozen bag of peas, trying to keep it from falling, I position my wrist on the pillow beside me. I feel Devin's body on my back as he sits and watches the muted TV. I let my high take over and quickly fall into a deep, drug-induced sleep.

Chapter 5

Sprain, Pain, Panic

A spine-chilling scream pierces the silence of night. I open my swollen eyes and attempt to focus. Disoriented, I sit up and wait for the room to stop spinning. I hear it again. It's Nate. Poor kid is having another nightmare.

His parents have told me he wakes up hollering in fright at least three times a week. I don't know what he dreams. Nate only confides in me that they are bad or scary. The Miller's family doctor, Dr. Robin Linghour, assures Nate's parents that he is going through a phase that will soon pass. Months have gone by, and nothing has changed. Personally, I think there must be a reason for him to continue having these awful dreams, but I keep it to myself. It's not my place to say.

The red alarm clock reads 4 am. Panic sets in. I passed out before calling home. Mom and I made a pact six years ago to let the other know if we aren't going to be home when we're expected. It hasn't been broken … until now. *I'm so mad at myself!*

Not Enough

Devin is lying on the bed beside me, sound asleep and snoring. I don't know how, but Nate's screaming episodes don't rattle him.

I need to get home in a hurry! I have no time to talk, listen to apologies, or engage in *make-him-feel-better* sex. Holding my breath, I climb over him and off the bed. Devin grumbles, turns onto his back, slides his hand down his boxers, and adjusts his manhood. I stand silent next to the bed and pray he won't wake up. When he begins to snore again, I thank God, tiptoe into the bathroom, and close the door behind me. Splashing cold water on my face I'm shocked into a state of consciousness, fit to drive.

I gather my things, ease the bedroom door open and listen for activity downstairs. All is quiet. I creep down the stairs without a sound. I figure Mr. and Mrs. Miller are busy comforting Nate. They tell him sweet and fanciful stories about puppies and lollipops to help him fall asleep again.

The bottom of the staircase is next to the front door. I strain to see as far as I can into the darkened house. A large figure passes through the hallway. As Penny would say, it scared the "bah-Jesus" out of me! My heart skips a beat or two and my lungs gasp for air. After waiting several minutes, I convince myself that the shadowy figure was Mr. Miller, and the coast is clear to leave. I open the front door and slip out unnoticed. Making up for the beats it missed, my heart is pounding to a drum line.

Brooks

Remembering the incident from last night, I know the engine does not need to be running for the car to move. I get in, release the emergency brake, and shift to neutral. Effortlessly, my car rolls down the driveway and onto the street. Of course, without the engine running, I have no power steering. Turning the wheel as hard as I can, I barely miss the Miller's mailbox as my back tires hit the street. *That would've been just ducky, my escape botched by mailbox slaughter.* When my car stops rolling, I'm a couple of houses down the street. I start the engine and head home.

Mom must be a worried mess!

Chapter 6
Doc-in-a-Box

Back at Parkview Terrace, I pull into one of the two parking spaces in front of our house. Mom's bedroom light is on. I hate that I'm going to lie, but I have no choice. I can't let her know what happened. What am I going to tell her? *Shit, this sucks!*

I take a deep breath and walk to the door. Mom is halfway down the stairs when I step inside.

"Rose! Where have you been?" I see her eyes are red and glassy. She's either been up crying or smoking weed. The latter is highly unlikely, at least not since the eighties. Mom told me she met a man at a party one night who smoked a joint with her laced with PCP and sinister intent. If she hadn't thrown up all over herself after smoking it, she would have been raped that night. I don't know why the guy didn't get sick, but I'm glad Mom puked!

"I'm sorry I didn't call, Mom. We were watching *Batman Returns* with Danny DeVito playing Penguin. You know I love Danny DeVito, but we fell asleep before it was over."

Brooks

"Rose, we made a deal ..."

I cut her off. "I know, Mom, and I'm sorry I worried you. I feel awful, and guilty, and disappointed in myself for disappointing you. I promise, promise, promise it won't happen again!"

"You had me so worried," she sobs before wrapping her arms around me. Cheek to cheek, I feel one of her tears trickle down my face.

Breaking the hug to hold my hands, she notices my swollen wrist.

"Holy crap! What happened?"

"It's not a big deal. Really, Mom, it's not. I was in Devin's room, and he was teaching me a wrestling move from that stupid show he watches. When I tried it on him, I lost my balance and slammed my wrist on the brass doorknob. But seriously, Mom, it looks worse than it feels."

"Oh, baby girl, who do you think you're kidding? If you fell off a ten-story building and broke every bone in your body, you'd still say you're okay. You've been that way since you were little. And how many bones have you broken? Good Lord! Look at that thing! Did you ice it? Hold tight, I'll go get something from the freezer."

She's right, I'm clumsy. I've broken both of my ankles and wrists, an elbow, and a few toes, but not once did I insist on seeing a doctor.

Mom returns with a bag of frozen lima beans, tying it around my wrist with a pair of old pantyhose. She's clever that way. Having been raised with six sisters and a modest family income, my mother learned to be thrifty.

Not Enough

"Wait right here, Rose, I need to find my keys."

Within minutes, we're at the 24-hour Doc-in-a-Box. Three hours later, my wrist has been x-rayed and dressed with a half-cast and elastic bandage. A nurse ushers us to an empty room where we wait to see a doctor.

For as long as I can remember, Mom acts so goofy in a doctor's office. This morning is no different. Before the doctor walks in, she grabs two of those black plastic covers they stick onto the flashlight to look into your ears or down your throat. Giggling, she sticks them into her bra. She looks like she has the longest, most pointed nipples in the world! Madonna has nothing on Mom! She puts on a pair of exam gloves, looks at me seriously, and says, "Bend over, young lady, or you get no lollipop."

We are cracking up when the doctor enters the room. Luckily, Dr. Alders has a sense of humor and starts laughing with us. Being subtle as always, Mom orders the doctor to "bend over." He declines but continues to chuckle. Mom steps behind the privacy curtain and removes her fake nipples. The doctor regains his composure and thanks Mom for adding humor to his morning.

Dr. Alders tells us my diagnosis. My wrist is sprained and has a hairline fracture. He hands me a prescription and sends us on our way. Before we leave, Mom stuffs a handful of gloves in her purse for future hair dying. I read the prescription.

Vicodin ... score!

Chapter 7
Principals Get Horny Too

Back home, after consuming a drive-through breakfast from Hardee's, Mom kisses me on my cheek and leaves to get my medicine. I grab a bag of frozen corn and head upstairs to bed.

My wrist is killing me. I take off my dirty clothes with my good hand and put on my softest pajamas. Like my bedspread, they're yellow with purple roses and dancing butterflies. When I wear them, I feel like a kid and take pleasure blending with my blanket.

Lying in bed, my mind is held hostage by thoughts of lies and abuse. I'm exhausted, but sleep won't come. I try a technique I read about stress-relief. I close my eyes and imagine a black wall. I try to erase my thoughts by painting each one of them onto the wall and let them disappear into the darkness. It's not helping.

My mental health is getting flushed down the toilet and I can't take much more. Right now, the lies I told Mom are tormenting me most. It's not like I never lied to her before. I'm not proud of it, but I never thought it made me a bad person. I rationalized by telling myself that everyone lies sometimes.

I hear soft tapping on my bedroom door.

"Come in, Mom."

"I've got your pain medicine." She hands me two tablets and a glass of water.

"Thanks, Mom."

"You're welcome, sweetheart. I'm leaving for work in an hour and won't be home 'til late. You gonna be, okay?"

"Yes ... no worries here." *Luckily, I'm playing it off like I'm telling the truth.* "Have a great night. And you look stunning, by the way."

"Thank you! There's a big sale tonight."

Mom is a knock-out. With the tall slim figure of a supermodel, perky boobs, long blonde hair, speckled brown hazel eyes, and a face resembling Marilyn Monroe, she's the caliber of pretty that makes other women want to look like her. She sells cosmetics and gives free makeovers. She always does well.

"I'm certain you'll do great, Mom. See you tonight." *I am so ready to be alone.*

"Okay, Rose, I love you. Now get some rest."

I'm all mixed up and filled with shame. I thought my lying days were long gone. Rest won't be easy.

***

Brooks

I was fourteen and nearing the end of my freshman year. Gabby and I skipped our morning classes. I had a dentist appointment that afternoon and Mom was picking me up at one o'clock. If I got back to school before then, I'd be in the clear. I suppose I didn't think it through very well. And I didn't foresee Mom coming early!

Before that day, I was good at skipping school. I knew if I showed up for homeroom to say "here" I would be counted as present, and the school secretary wouldn't call my house at the end of the day. Even if I missed all my other classes, they wouldn't call. I mean, they took attendance, but it wasn't reported daily. So, what did I care?

It was noon when we got back to school. I knew I made it with time to spare. Until, Annie, from homeroom, told me Mrs. Schelding, the school attendance officer, had been calling me to the office for the last hour. I was cold busted. No lies could save me. *Fuck!* I wanted to bail but I begrudgingly walked to the principal's office.

I opened the office door, and there was Mrs. Schelding, wearing bright red lipstick and a smug expression. Shifting her focus to Principal Bailey's open door, she announced with a crooked smile, "Rose Moon is here ..."

Mom was sitting in the office. She looked angry.

"Well, hello, Rose. I'm so glad you decided to join us today," Principal Bailey said in his customary condescending tone. "Take a seat. Your mother and I have a lot to discuss with you." *Awesome.*

My class attendance sheets spread from one end of

his giant oak desk to the other for Mom to see. Principal Bailey directed me to sit on the chair closest to the wall by the green metal filing cabinets ... the interrogation room! The only thing missing was the bright light in my face. Didn't matter, I was sweating.

Mom was restless on her chair beside me. She was tapping her toes and shaking her head in disbelief.

"Rose Riley Moon," Mom stammered. "Where on God's green earth have you been?"

"Not here." *Bad answer.*

Mom raised her voice, "Yes, I'm quite aware of that, Rose. Now is not the time to be a smart ass. Answer my question. Where have you been?"

"Not here." *Damn, I said it again.*

Really, there was no other way to answer the question. Was I supposed to admit that I was riding around with friends smoking weed?

"Rose," Principal Bailey calmly interrupted, "would you do us all a favor and save time by answering your mother's question?"

This time, I kept my "smart ass" mouth shut. Unfortunately, silence also did not work.

"Okay Rose, you sit there and say nothing," Mom barked. "While you were *not here,* Mr. Bailey and I had time to get acquainted."

"So, you gonna start dating him now?" *What is wrong with me?*

The principal shot back, "That's enough young lady. You will not disrespect your mother in my presence. I advise you to think before you speak." I could see Bailey was flustered. He was having a tough time averting his attention from Mom's perky boobs. His face was flushed, and his upper lip was sweating. *I hope my looks have that power someday.*

Bailey was right. I was being a disrespectful brat. The seriousness of the situation made me assume the defensive-hostile-teenage approach of reacting. I sat as they reviewed my records. Mom took a small notepad from her purse and a pen from the "Principal of the Year" mug on the desk. She wrote as Bailey recited:

"Seventeen absences in Earth Science. Twenty-one in Basic Algebra. You were absent nineteen times in U.S. History, nineteen in English 111 ... and you missed study hall twenty-six times. However, Introduction to Drawing ... zero absences."

From behind his enormous desk, Bailey cut his eyes at me.

"That, Rose," he said with a smirk, "is a grand total of one hundred and two missed classes." He paused, looking curiously at his notes. "No absences in art? Interesting that you made it to art class but not the others. Anything to say about that?"

"I like art. And study hall's a joke." *That about summed it up.*

Mom clenched her teeth, her eyes like daggers. "Rose, we'll discuss this further at home."

I stood up and snapped back, "Fine, Mom, whatever!"

What I wanted to say was that there must have been a mistake ... I'll confess to missing a lot of classes, but one hundred and two seems rather exorbitant, even for me.

On the way to the dentist, we didn't speak. Her exaggerated huffing and puffing was annoying. I'd never seen her that mad. Ironically, we got to the dental office right on time. To my benefit, Mom had time to cool down while she waited.

At school, I was sentenced to ten grueling days of in-school suspension. I sat in the ISS classroom with my fellow trouble-making peers all day long. We were allowed to do two things: schoolwork and breathe. Fortunately, the supervising teacher was lazy and stayed at his desk all day reading the newspaper and solving crossword puzzles. I mostly wrote poems and drew flowers. Not being able to sneak out for a cigarette was the worst part.

Ten days later, I was released from ISS and integrated back to my normal schedule. But, for the remainder of the year, I had to carry an attendance card to every class for my teachers to sign. At the end of each day, I gave the card to Mrs. Schelding, the self-appointed mistress of forgery detection, and she would use her divine power to dismiss me from school.

At home, my punishment was much worse. I had to live in the presence of my mother's disappointment.

Chapter 8
An Outstanding Pupil

*A*fter my big bust at school, Mom started snooping through my stuff. It wasn't long before she found something she wished she hadn't. In my bottom dresser drawer, tucked into a stray sock, were rolling papers, a glass pipe, and a bag of weed. How could I have been so careless? The look of disappointment in Mom's eyes coupled with an absolute lack of trust.

I had to "pay the price" for my actions and I didn't like that one bit. Mom joined a support group for parents of "troubled" teenagers. And my punishment began. Each new drug-detecting method Mom learned from her fellow "concerned" parents was immediately put into practice. I kept my mouth shut and went along with it, but I was becoming resentful.

Ironically, the drug that concerned Mom the most, LSD, was also my drug of choice. To add a psychedelic twist to a typically mundane life, tripping on acid provides an escape, an adventure … both. A hit of acid makes the world an amusement park of colored flashing lights and fluorescent trails, while the ground is moving in rhythm to your heartbeat, and your best friend's face morphs into a tree frog... or Cinderella. Even if you're exactly where you were when you get back from your trip, it was still a tasty vacation. *I miss it sometimes.*

Mom didn't know I was using until she found a note folded up in the side pocket of my book bag:

> Hey Gabbs,
> FYI, I hooked up with a couple hits for the weekend ... Woodstock! Can't wait! LSD baby ... bring on the show! Meet me at lunch. Love ya Chickie!
>   – Rose

When Mom found that note, it sunk in that I need to stop hiding shit when I'm high. Because, apparently, I'm not particularly good at it. And I'm awfully forgetful.

Mom had no firsthand knowledge of the effects of LSD. She only knew what she was told in the group. The other parents seemed to overdramatize all the topics they discussed. Mom told me someone claimed the little slips of paper soaked in acid were substances of the Devil's doing. *Bible-thump, much? Geez ...*

Mom did learn some legit ways to detect LSD use. For example, when an individual is high on acid their pupils nearly eclipse the iris and won't retract normally in light. Luckily, I have very deep brown eyes, and passing a flashlight test was a breeze, whether I was tripping or not. But I wasn't going to be the one to educate Mom on that!

When I came home at night, Mom conducted her delightful *did you or did you not use drugs* testing routine. First, I had to pass the flashlight test. *Easy, next …*

Mom had me close my eyes with both arms stretched out to my sides and then touch my nose with each hand. Next, I walked a straight line where the seam of the vinyl kitchen floor met the carpeted dining room. Someone in her group must have been a cop. She smelled my breath for alcohol, smelled my clothes for weed, and searched my purse for paraphernalia. Afterward, Mom gave me a hug and sent me to bed with a sweet and sincere, "I love you."

Little did she know, after gaining clearance to proceed upstairs, I spent many nights camped out in my bathroom with the window open and the fan on, writing in my journal by candlelight, and smoking the weed I hid in a hole on the side of my mattress… finally, a good stash spot! I saw it on a documentary about jail. *Prisoners are clever.* I kinda felt bad for Mom. All those tests and she remained clueless.

To further battle my drug use, Mom made me see a therapist. Twice a week, for three months, I saw Dr. Menendez, and was expected to tell him everything on my mind. *Not happening!* I was there against my will, and I didn't trust him. But after the ninth or tenth speech he gave about doctor-patient confidentiality, I began to believe he was serious about keeping my secrets secret.

Once Dr. Menendez earned my trust, oddly enough, I found comfort in having someone to talk to about life and its many facets, honestly and openly, without regrets or repercussions. He didn't encourage my unruly behavior but seemed to understand my point of view and mostly took my side ... the only side he was hearing.

On the second visit of each week, I peed in a cup while Mom watched so I couldn't tamper with the sample. Not that I even knew how. I did hear that drinking vinegar cleaned out your system. And after trying it, Dr. Menendez told me it was a myth. I wished he'd shared that tidbit of information earlier. That shit was fucking nasty! From then on, I drank a gallon of water before my appointments and crossed my fingers. Luckily, I always passed.

Brutal best describes the last condition of my punishment. I was forbidden to hang out with friends who drank or did drugs ... that would be everybody. And making new friends at Grand Landing High School wasn't a possibility. The established cliques were deep-rooted. The day I befriended the cheerleading squad or the debate team, for instance, would be the day that unicorns flew out of my asshole and were sold as family pets. Those students wouldn't want to be friends with me, anyhow. I was deep-rooted in the party clique.

Much to my satisfaction, it didn't take long to wear Mom down. After a couple of weeks of my whining and crying over not seeing Devin and Gabby, she caved. I gave her immense gratitude and a promise to tighten up. Gradually, I earned back her trust, and life pretty much went back to normal. *Mom can be so naive.*

Chapter 9
Beauty and the Buzz

Bored and loopy from the pain medicine, I lay on my bed watching cars pass by and counting how many people drive with their hands on top of the steering wheel and how many on the bottom. I hear the front door close behind Mom. Her burgundy Thunderbird with the "Have you hugged your child today?" bumper sticker passes under my window. She has both hands on top. That makes thirty-nine.

I close the curtains, slide off my bed, and shuffle down the stairs. Passing the mother-daughter portraits on the stairway wall, I'm filled with joy. I'm so lucky to have Mom! She's the nicest person I've ever known, and she gives me respect, patience, understanding, and unconditional love. Right now, I'm also over the moon in love with Dr. Alders for prescribing me Vicodin. *I don't recall seeing a ring on his finger.*

Downstairs, I turn on the TV and grab a cold Pepsi from the fridge. The pills make me feel like I've been snacking on cotton balls … but it's worth it. Actually, cotton is a delicacy in some regions of the world. Or maybe that's whale blubber ... or hog balls. I laugh. I have no idea what I'm talking to myself about, but if consuming cotton balls made me feel like I do right now, they'd be on the menu daily! Wait, I'm no addict ... on the menu once a week.

On the kitchen table, in our red spiral-bound notebook, a note from Mom reminds me to call. Our answering machine is blinking red. Seven messages. I need to call Mom first, so I ignore it. I take the pantyhose from tying the frozen bag of veggies to my wrist and wrap it around my head and over my mouth. I get through to her direct line.

"Thank you for calling Leggett's, your number one source for the finest cosmetics. My name is Randy. How may I help you this evening?"

Disguised by pantyhose, I use my best little old lady voice, "Yes, hello dear. I'm calling to ask if you sell a cold cream product for your, well, for your ... your ass, dear?"

"Cold cream for your ... ass, you say?" Mom whispers into the phone.

"Oh, no, no, no ... I'm sorry, dear. Did I say cold cream? Oh, silly me. I meant cover-up. Cover-up for your ass. One you can use to hide unsightly pimples. Adult diapers are wreaking havoc on my cheeks." *I can't believe I'm pulling this off! Pantyhose really is handy for all sorts of things!*

Mom is using her best-skilled voice. "I understand. They really are rough on the skin. I'm so sorry you're having this problem." *Oh my God. Now she's pretending she can relate! This is as good as it gets!* "We have plenty of foundations and powders that should work fine on your... well, on your ass, ma'am."

"That is wonderful, dear. I'm so glad I called."

"Yes, ma'am, I am here to help. We're gonna get you all fixed up. Now, tell me, do you have any issues with sensitive skin?"

Maintaining my granny voice, I say, "No, dear. I don't have any problems with sensitive skin." I unwrap the pantyhose from around my mouth. "I do however have an issue with your gullibility!" I burst into laughter.

"Rose! I could kill you ... you really had me! Cover-up for my ass. Good grief, how do you come up with this stuff?" She lets out a high-pitched laugh and then shushes herself.

"I'm sorry, Mom, I couldn't resist. You asked me to call but you didn't specify what to say."

"I asked you to call so I could find out how you're doing, smarty-pants." *She called me that growing up. It makes me smile.* "But you seem to be doing rather good. How is your wrist?"

I tell her the painkillers took the edge off and helped me sleep, but I still hurt like hell. Honestly, it's not that bad right now, but I'm ready to take another pill. Life is cheery for the first time in days.

"Aw, I'm sorry sweetheart. At least you're in good humor ... you crazy girl!" Mom chuckles softly. "I left the bottle by the kitchen sink." *I know, I have sixteen left.* "Be sure to eat first. And keep your wrist iced and elevated. There's a bag of peas in the freezer."

"Okay, Mom ... will do."

"Alrighty. I need to get back to work. I see a customer approaching, face screaming for help. I love you. I'll be home around 10:30."

"I'll be here. Have a great night, Mom. Love you, too!"

I hang up the phone, swallow another pill, take a deep breath, and press play on the answering machine. The first three messages are Devin. I hear his voice and hit delete. I have no words for him right now. I am pissed off, sad, hurt, upset, confused, and need time to process my emotions! I'll talk to him when I'm ready. *Abusive, fucking dickhead!*

I think Devin has been getting back at me, with his ugliness and rejection, for breaking his heart years ago. It makes sense. I should've noticed it earlier, but I was set on making it right. Now, there's not one right thing about it.

The next three calls are hang-ups. And the last is Gabby. There's no predicting what her silly ass will say. I listen to the message:

"Rose, Rose, Rose, I know you pick your nose! It's Gabby, Gabby, Bo-Babby! Where are you, my pretty little pet? I need to talk! Call me back, Nose Picker, or I will be forced to call you more-ore-ore! Seriously, call me back. I have a question. Love you! Bye!"

We're both eighteen, but Gabby acts like a little kid sometimes. It tends to drive me batty, but I love her, nonetheless. She's the only friend I can be myself around. Despite our differences in personality and general ways of thinking, we have a lot of fun together. And, we've never had a stupid girl fight.

Gabby answers on the first ring. "Hi, hey, hello!"

"Hey, goofy-ass! This is the nose picker calling."

She laughs, "thanks for taking your finger out of your nose long enough to dial my number. You're so sweet."

"Yep, that's me, a nose-picking sweetheart! What are you up to?"

"I have a surprise!" She sounds super excited.

I match her energy, "I love surprises! What is it? Did you buy me a new car? Did ya? Did ya? Huh? Huh? Huh?"

"No! Good wishful thinking, though!"

"Well, shit, that sucks. I had my heart set on a new car! Did you win the lottery?"

"No, I didn't win the lottery, but I kinda feel like I did." Gabby says softly. *She's confusing me.* "I told you it's a surprise." *She's excited again. Okay …*

"Well, for fuck's sake, Gabbs, tell me the surprise!"

"No."

"No?" Pain killers are getting me through this tedious conversation. "What do you mean, no?"

"I mean, I don't want to tell you over the phone. It's a big deal! Do you work tomorrow night?"

She sounds frustrated with me. *That's new.* I bend my voice to sound soft and patient, "nope, sure don't. I have the whole weekend off. What's going on, Gabby? Are you alright?"

"I'm great!"

I don't quite believe her. "Sincerely?"

"Yes, Rose, sincerely."

"Okay, good. I'm excited to hear what's up. What do you have in mind?"

She exhales heavily. "Tomorrow is a league night, and Jordan will be at the bowling alley. So, I was thinking I could come hang out at your place for a while."

I forgot that Gabby's new boyfriend is a bowler. When I found out, I thought, wow, what a fucking nerd. Then I met him and thought, wow, what a good-looking fucking nerd!

"Works for me." This is a perfect time to tell my bullshit story. "I thought you were gonna ask me to go bowling, I'm glad I was wrong. I hurt myself last night."

"You did? Oh no, Rose, what happened?"

I pull the phone away from my ear, take a deep breath, and tell her the same bullshit story I told Mom.

"Ah, shit! That's terrible, Rose! I'm so sorry. You are forever hurting yourself … did the doctor give you anything for pain?"

"Yes, but he only gave me ten pills." *I have no plans of sharing.*

"That's all?" Gabby sounds disappointed.

I'm ready to get off the phone. "Yep, that's all. So anyway, what time should I expect you, chickie?"

"I'm off work at 6:30, so 7:00 good?"

"Perfect. See you then."

We hang up and I look at the clock; it's nine-thirty. Mom won't be home for at least an hour. I pack a bowl and go out back to smoke. Our patio is a ten-by-ten-foot slab of concrete surrounded by a six-foot-high privacy fence. We have a small glass table, two wicker chairs, eight potted plants, and a small, boxed garden.

Mom loves her patio garden. She grows everything from tomatoes and squash to cucumbers and cabbage. Our private patio serves as my mom's sanctuary and tending to the plants is her therapy. *I mainly use it to get high.*

I sit back in the wicker chair painted purple and hit my bowl until my eyes turn red. I light a cigarette and get lost in thought ... I wonder if people who are at ease in the world have confidence because they've been reincarnated enough times to have a handle on how the world works. And, if so, perhaps people with anxiety, like me, struggle through life because they are living their first rodeo. Rodeo ... what a weird word. Wait, weird is a weird word. It's spelled wrong. Rules of grammar, people ... "I before E except after C" ... it should be wierd ... and even weard sounds more correct than weird. This world makes no sense.

I get up and smile at the plants. "See you guys and girls later," I say sweetly. "Happy blooming!" Mom would be pleased.

Lying on the couch, I look for something worth watching on TV. With a good buzz, it's easy to get interested in almost anything. Perfect, the mating rituals of the honeybee. The few lucky drones that get to mate with the queen are instantly killed and left for dead when their testicles explode at climax. The dead drone's penis stays inside the queen to be used as a blockade, preventing any other drone from fertilizing her eggs. *Brutal … fascinating.*

Chapter 10

My Best Friend is a Basket Case

Gabby and I are from broken homes but with one major difference ... her mom left. That's ass backward. The father is the fuck-up who ditches his family. I cannot comprehend a mother capable of abandoning her baby.

When Gabby was five years old, her dad, John Thomas, was arrested for robbing a liquor store and was sentenced to six years in County Jail. During this time, Gabby was sent to live with her Aunt Liz.

The night Gabby told me about her aunt, we were at my house, drinking my mom's wine, and sharing secrets we'd collected over the years. To start, Gabby told me that Liz thought children were "irritating and needy little shits who waste money and get in the way." She rarely had clean clothes or shoes that fit. Nurturing of any kind was non-existent, and Gabby was often left to care for herself when she was hungry, cold, or sad.

Liz bled Southern Comfort and Coke and was drunk most of the time. At age seven, Gabby learned how to stand on a stool and cook scrambled eggs. She said there were always pieces of shell in them, but it was food in her belly when her aunt was passed out drunk. This explains why Gabby won't eat eggs.

Apparently, Liz had a revolving door of men in her life. Gabby said it seemed like a different man every month. And when her latest affair didn't pan out, she blamed Gabby and took it out on her ... violently. Liz dragged Gabby around the house by her hair, yelling at her, and calling her things like a "worthless dirty pig" and a "stupid little bitch." This carried on until Liz found a new dickhead to drink with and fuck.

Before serving time, Mr. Thomas was sweet to Gabby. They played Barbies and explored nature in their backyard. He brushed her hair, watched cartoons with her in the mornings, and read bedtime stories each night. Gabby held on to the dream of feeling special and loved again.

When her dad was released, Gabby told me in a whisper, he started to drink more and use cocaine. He became distant and angry. Gabby did all the household chores and was left to fend for herself, again. She felt like her dad didn't love her anymore. I can't imagine how painful that is. Mom taught me that love between a parent and child should feel like the sun shining on both sides, not searching in the sewer for a rainbow.

About halfway through the bottle of wine, and a box of tissues, Gabby started feeling better. She finally let go of all the pain she held for so many years. She had a glow about her and a sense of calm. She released herself from the suffering. It was a beautiful thing.

Growing up, Mom gave me love and moral support. She boosted my self-confidence and made me believe I could accomplish anything. No one did that for Gabby. Low self-esteem has plagued her throughout life and continues to influence her consistent series of poor decisions.

Gabby's search for the love she was denied by her father consumes her. Since the day we met, finding a boy to love her has been her top priority, above all else, including schoolwork. She managed to squeak through middle school, but high school was more of a challenge. I helped, in my own way, by letting her cheat off my tests. But, after a while, it got old, and her lack of effort began to annoy me. Instead of waking her up to copy my answers before the bell rang, I let her sleep. She wasn't upset with me about it, but I admit, I was riddled with guilt when she dropped out of school halfway through our junior year.

Anyway, when it comes to boyfriends, Gabby isn't picky. Anyone she meets with the needs she requires is given a fair chance. *Basically, anyone with a penis who shows interest.* Jordan, her current boyfriend, is her most recent mistake. I want to believe that he won't cause permanent scars on her already brittle heart. But, in the three short months they've dated, I've witnessed enough to know he's an untrustworthy asshole! And I don't know how to tell Gabby without hurting her.

***

Brooks

I see headlights from my bedroom window. It's seven o'clock. Gabby's here. I hurry to the kitchen, take another pain pill, and toss the bottle in the silverware drawer. I open the door before she knocks. Had I looked through the peephole, I'd have seen the bouquet of flowers she was holding. But I didn't and now they're on the ground.

"Oh no! I'm sorry, Gabbs!"

"Holy crap! You scared the shit outta me!" She laughs and bends down to pick up the flowers.

"Aw, you brought me get well flowers ... how sweet." I take the flowers from her and smell the fresh blooms. "Thank you, chickie!"

"You're welcome, my sweet Rose. But don't over-do the appreciation, I did use my employee discount ... all five fingers of it." Gabby smiles with the satisfaction of doing a good deed. I am blown away. She's never done anything like this. *Usually, it's all about her.*

Gabby cuts the stems and I place each one in a vase. The myriad of colors brings life to the predominately brown kitchen.

"Devin didn't even get me a card."

"Really? What's up with that?" Gabby asks with disdain.

"He's a dick." We laugh.

"I brought you something to help kill the pain, too." She looks at me with a wicked grin, unzips her purse, and pulls out a joint from her cigarette pack.

I'm buzzed already but see no harm in enhancing it. Anything to block reality is on the table. "You're fucking

53

awesome, Gabbs! Wanna step out back and spark it up?"

"What do you think, Rose? Duh!"

"Oh, shut up! Come on, let's go." I lead the way.

Gabby's been here a whole ten minutes and hasn't mentioned her surprising news. It's unusual, but I guess she'll tell me when she's ready. In the meantime, I intend to enjoy my buzz and not bring it up. *It's nice having it all about me for a change.*

Sitting out on the patio, Gabby lights the joint. I'm beyond high when she tells me Jordan called her at work and asked her to bring his gloves to the bowling alley.

"Rose, you don't mind running up to the bowling alley with me real quick to drop off Jordan's gloves, do you? It'll only take a minute." Gabby bats her eyes at me.

My initial reaction would normally be a speedy and resounding "no." I've never even been inside a bowling alley and I'm not a fan of Jordan, at all. My anxiety prevents me from venturing out of my comfort zone. But the pain pills have temporarily remedied my disorder. Much to Gabby's surprise, I respond, "Absolutely, let's do it!"

Chapter 11
Twinkle-Toes-Rose

T he parking lot at Shakey's Bowling Alley is packed. I had no idea knocking pins over by hurling a ball at them is so popular.

Circling the lot for an open space, we watch a group of folks, wearing different colored jerseys, standing next to the metal benches out front. They're drinking from red plastic cups, comparing scores, and calling each other liars. A portly man in a tie-dyed shirt throws his beer in the face of the smallest guy there. Security guards pin down the asshole and usher him off the property while the little guy laughs and mocks him.

I turn my attention to Gabby, "Wow, this is a classy joint, right here."

"Oh, shut up, Rose! Don't pretend like you didn't enjoy the show!"

"You're right. You got me. Finest family entertainment ever!"

The left side of the red cinderblock building is lined with men wearing cowboy hats, denim jeans, boots, and orange jerseys with a silhouette of a galloping mustang on the front pocket. I wonder if their bowling shoes have mini spurs on them.

"What do you think, Gabbs?"

"What do I think about what, Rose?"

"What I just asked."

"You didn't ask anything."

"Yes, I did!"

"Oh my God, Rose, are you serious? You didn't say anything."

"Well, shit, I thought I did."

"Ha ha! Okay, what is it you thought you asked?"

"Umm ... oh shit. I forget ... something to do with horses, I think."

Gabby's jealous, "I sure do wish you had enough of those pills to share."

I ignore the comment.

Gabby double parks behind Jordan's truck while we wait. We watch a family of five, wearing purple, white, and green jerseys, take bowling balls out of their minivan. Everyone has a nickname embroidered on the front of their jersey. Cheesy ones like Queen-Of-The-Lane-Jane and Gutter-Ball-Barb. As declared on the back of their jerseys, together, they are the "Rock-N-Roll" bowlers.

Gabby turns to me, "So, Twinkle-Toes-Rose, you ready to do some bowling?"

"You know it, Not-Too-Shabby-Gabby!"

My mind is momentarily consumed by how the parents got their kids to wear those costumes in public.

But after watching their interaction, I start to feel sad and wish I had a goofy family who did corny things together. I shrug it off. I feel too good to fuck up my buzz with sad shit.

Finally, an empty space. Gabby pulls in, turns off the ignition, and puts Jordan's gloves in her purse. I mist myself with a spray of Liz Claiborne perfume. Choking on the fumes that went up my nose and in my mouth, Gabby's laughing at me. In retaliation, I spray it again in her direction. It goes up her nose too!

"Take that, Miss Laffy McLafferson! Ha!"

"You bitch ... that was cold up!" she wails between sneezes.

The thing I love most about our friendship is how we can playfully fuck with each other and not get mad. "Bitch" is often used as a term of endearment.

We get out of the car, and I start skipping toward the building. *Damn, I feel good!* Gabby catches up with me and we skip, hand in hand, to the entrance. Inside, Gabby steps away to bring Jordan his gloves, and I hit a concrete wall of chaos. With people bowling, playing pool and arcade games, changing shoes, eating, drinking, and being loud, this place is fucking nuts! Normally, I would be paralyzed with anxiety. *Dr. Alders, will you marry me?*

The interior is massive. Bowling lanes are lined up against the back wall. There are thirty-five of them, divided by ball return belts with blinking lights, point-keeping stations, and lots of orange chairs bolted to the floor. I have a sudden inclination to run down a lane and slide into the pins.

The arcade and pool tables are on the right. I see colors moving around on the video game screens and feel like I dropped acid. A snack bar, tables, and booths are on the left. The smell of popcorn and nachos fill the air. My stomach growls but I don't want to eat and lose my buzz.

The shoe rental area is to the left of the entrance. Behind the counter are cubby holes filled with used shoes from floor to ceiling. Wearing old shoes that had a slew of dirty socks and stinky feet in them deters me from the sport altogether.

Blaring out from four speakers, dance music is pounding to the pulse of the alley. I start moving to the music. When Gabby comes back, I'm dancing. Her eyes get wide, and her mouth drops open. This is the first time I've ever danced in public. We've never been out when I didn't need a few drinks and an hour to get my bearings before I could breathe again, much less dance.

This place is painted with the most dazzling strokes of diversity. On the side walls, are two of the most beautiful murals I've ever seen.

On the left is a landscape view of a tropical island with white sand glistening in the reflection of the sun's rays. Graceful palm trees are painted to look like they're swaying in the gentle breeze of the warm Caribbean wind. The leaves on the trees break up the gleaming white sand with shadows that lead to clear blue water. I want to live in this painting.

Brooks

On the right wall is a majestic waterfall cascading down from a lofty mountain shrouded in a misty haze. The water below creates a pool with tall grasses and a gathering of crimson and yellow wildflowers. In the distance, a small lagoon offers refuge to migrating birds.

The scenes are calming amid the mayhem. I'm reminded of posters my mother and I had on our walls when I was a kid. We dreamed of going to places like these someday. Who knew all we had to do was take a trip to the bowling alley?

Gabby takes my hand and leads me darting back and forth around the tables, dodging kids running around holding hot dogs and cheese nachos, and servers carrying mugs of beer and plastic baskets of pretzels. David, the concession stand worker, has a major crush on Gabby, so he doesn't card her for beer. She gets a pitcher, and we sit at a table closest to the waterfall. I thought we were here just to drop off Jordan's gloves. Good thing I'm in a highly altered state of mind. If not, I'd be awfully agitated.

Gabby pours me a drink and I light a cigarette. Being responsible, I shouldn't be drinking on top of the weed and pain killers. I debate with myself as to whether I'm responsible or not. Undecided, I choose not to partake. I'm plenty high to enjoy this circus of chaos.

I really need to pee, so I scan the walls for the women's restroom. It's hard to miss with the big-ass pink, fluorescent light above the door. Walking back to the table, I see Jordan and his bowling buddies. I'm relieved they're wearing matching blue button-down shirts without goofball names on them or a glittery bowling ball with flames shooting out of it on the back.

"Hey, Rose, how are you doin' tonight?" Jordan asks, eyeing me up and down.

"I'm doing just fine, Jordan. Thanks."

"Well, you're looking fine as usual. Isn't she Gabby?" He gives her a soft jab with his elbow, and then softly pats her belly.

"Beautiful as ever." Gabby blows me a kiss.

"Okay, okay, thank you both! Now, let's move on with our lives," I say, feeling uneasy.

Jordan introduces his bowling teammates to me as Bryan, LoJack, Heff, and Mitchell. We exchange quick hellos, and they each artfully check me out. You know, perhaps they should have a team name printed on the back of their shirts ... The Dandy Dickheads ... or something like that.

Jordan turns to Gabby. "Babe, we gotta get back to the game."

"Really? Already?"

"Yes, babe. Thank you for bringing my gloves."

"You're welcome. I guess I'll see you later... love you."

He kisses Gabby and walks back to the lanes.

Gabby watches him with sad eyes. She's truly in love with this asshole. I'm getting a headache, and my buzz is fading. It's time Gabby tells me her news.

"So, Gabby, are you gonna tell me your surprise, or what?"

"Yes, of course I am."

"Well, what are you waiting for? Are clowns gonna pop out of the bathroom singing show tunes and throwing balloon animals at us to heighten the excitement?"

"No, actually they will be driving into the building in tiny colorful cars before the singing and balloons. Thank you very much!"

"Alright! Now we're talking, Gabbs … bring in the clowns!"

"Rose, you're so stupid!" *She means that in a good way.*

"I know, that's why you love me."

"That, your beautiful brown eyes, and charming personality." Gabby says in a seductive tone.

"Oh, stop!" I laugh. "Enough of these childish antics!" I can't remember where I heard that, but I've been waiting for a chance to use it. "Spill it, Not-too-Shabby-Gabby!"

"Alright, Twinkle-Toes-Rose … here goes … I'm pregnant!"

Chapter 12

Sex, Lies, and Substance Abuse

Gabby and I share the desperately-seeking-love-by-baby syndrome. Having a baby will fill the hole in our hearts and make life happy and filled with joy, love, and sunshine. As pathetic and irrational as that may seem, it makes perfect sense to us.

"Rose, did you hear me? I'm pregnant."

In an instant, my buzz vanishes, and I'm thrust back into the realm of reality. "You're pregnant?" *The night was going so well.*

"Yes, Rose, for the third time, I'm pregnant!"

To my best ability, I feign happiness.

"Holy shit, Gabbs! I wasn't sure if I heard you right. Congratulations, that's incredible!" *Please let my trembling on the inside not be showing outwardly.*

"Well, thank you, Rose ... geez, for a second, I thought you weren't happy for me."

I take Gabby's cup of beer off the table and guzzle it. "Oh my God, no way, chickie ... I couldn't be happier!" *Fucking lies!* "How are you feeling? Are you sick in the mornings? Do your boobs hurt? I promise they look bigger!" I stop myself from running out of the building screaming and throwing shit.

"Oh my God, Rose, I feel great! Not getting sick, but, yes, my boobs are sore as fuck!" She feels herself up. "They are bigger, huh? I was hoping but wasn't sure."

"You're gonna be in a C cup before you know it!"

Gabby gets even more excited. "Bonus!"

"How does Jordan feel? Is he happy too?" I inquire with my bullshit-painted-on smile.

"He is, Rose! He's as excited as me! He had been holding me upside down over the side of the bed hoping gravity will help his sperm swim."

"For real? Wow! I'm so happy for you guys!"

"Thank you, my sweet Rose. I'm so excited!"

"I know! Me too!" *I'm gonna throw up.* "I hate to complain at such a joyous time, but my wrist is starting to throb." *Using my injury to my advantage. Thanks Devin … dick!* "Let's get outta here, momma."

I gather my things and hurry Gabby along. She's taking way too long saying goodbye. Come on, already!

Finally, back in the car, I practice deep breathing and smiling at the same time. It's more challenging than you'd think. With every bump on the road, I'm becoming more undone. My brain is burdened by Gabby's happy news of motherhood with a happy boyfriend and my unhappy possible pregnancy with an unhappy abusive asshole.

Trying not to sound sour, "does it worry you that you've only been together a few months?"

"Oh, no, not at all," she insists. "He is fully in love with me. He's different from the others. He's special. What we have is real love. And, Rose, I'm gonna be a mother ... the mom I never had. My baby will always feel loved. He's never gonna want for anything and will never, ever feel alone like I did. I'm gonna be a great mom!"

You're certainly off to a great start, smoking weed, drinking beer, and puffing on cigarettes.

We pass the strip mall where Devin's working at his parent's restaurant, *Sampson's Deli*. We haven't talked since Friday night, and I can't get him off my mind. Why does Gabby get to be so happy? Between my envy of her blissful pregnancy and my jealousy of her glee, I glance at the clock. It's only nine. The deli closes in an hour. I contemplate going.

We pull into Parkview Terrace. I just need to keep it together for a few more minutes. Gabby parks and I lean over, hug her, and give her a kiss on the cheek. Getting out of the car, the tears come. I'm glad Mom's working. I'm not ready to talk to her about any of this. I can't keep it from her forever. But I will for a while longer.

Sitting on the couch with car keys in hand, I'm torn. Fifteen minutes have passed since Gabby dropped me off. I can either stay here and cry myself to sleep or drive to the deli to see Devin. I don't think I can sit here alone and wallow. I'm manic as hell and can't slow my heart from racing. I need to see him and get it out of my system. I grab a pen and scribble a note for Mom.

Brooks

I get to my car, open the door, and my knees buckle from anxiety. With one hand on top of the open car door and the other planted on the roof, I sway and struggle to regain balance. Slowly, I steady myself enough to get in. Am I not caring about my own well-being? Maybe not. I shift to reverse and back out about three feet, then pull back in. *What the fuck am I doing?*

I can't be thinking clearly. I'm not stupid enough to chance vehicular death. I get out of my car and go back inside. The phone is ringing. Mom's probably running late and wants to check in. I can't sound like I've been crying. I blow my nose and clear my throat.

"Hello."

"Baby, I'm so glad you answered. I've been calling."

It's Devin. I'm relieved it's him, but I can't let him know that. "I haven't been up for talking."

Sweetly he says, "I understand, baby. I can't believe I hurt you like that. Will you ever forgive me? Oh God, Rose, I hope so. I can't live without you. Please don't leave me again."

I ignore his remarks. "Mom and I spent the entire morning at the Doc-in-a-Box. My wrist is fractured and badly sprained. It hurts like hell, and ..."

Devin cuts me off, "Oh my God. No. Fuck, baby ..."

I cut him off, "I don't know how long it's gonna take to heal, Devin. You really fucked it up."

He sighs heavily. "It will never happen again, Rose, I promise you, baby."

I hear him sniffle. Is he crying? I hope so. I want him to cry. To hurt.

"What did you tell your mom?" Devin asks in a whisper.

"Don't panic. I told her it was an accident. I said we were wrestling, and I hit it on the doorknob."

"Did she believe you?"

"Yes."

"Okay. I'll tell my parents the same."

"Sure, Devin, that's fine. Tell them whatever you want." I sound angry. *Good.*

"You have every right to be mad at me, baby. I'm mad at myself. Believe me, I am." He sniffles again.

"Okay, well, I'm exhausted, Devin, and in pain ... I need to hang up now."

"Thank you for answering baby. I love you."

I almost reciprocate his sentiment from habit but stop myself. Whether I still loved him or not, I can't give him reason to think everything's going to be fine after what he did. We hang up, and I wonder how long he's going to be sweet and contrite. When we first got together, Devin hurting me never crossed my mind.

Chapter 13

The Human Magnet

As a freshman in high school, I knew boys found me attractive. They weren't shy to show it. That's the power, I suppose, of a pretty face and big boobs. I have Mom to thank for that ... well, the pretty face part. The impressiveness of her breasts pales in comparison to mine. Regardless, I was incredibly shy and had no interest in letting any pathetic high school boy touch my heart or my double-Ds. Until Devin.

The first time I laid eyes on Devin Miller, my friends and I were outside, smoking cigarettes between classes, when we saw two boys running across the schoolyard chased by Big George, the senior security guard.

"You boys stop right now!" George panted loudly. He was older and had a large build, flab not muscle. No match for the young, adrenaline-pumped boys he was hollering at. "I know your names! You may get away today, but I'll get you tomorrow! Mark my words, boys!"

With intense interest, we watched the drama play out. As Devin passed, it was as if the chase turned into a slow-motion segment of an action film. He paused and smiled, and I took a mental picture. With just one look, he had my panties in a twist. He was hot, and I would make him mine!

When the world returned to normal speed, George gave up his pursuit. He stood, bent over at the waist, and using his knees as a crutch, trying to catch his breath. After struggling to return to an upright position, he began walking back, defeated.

For the remainder of the day, I fantasized about the striking guy who shook me to the core with his bright eyes and sexy smile. I learned his name, Devin Miller. He was a sophomore. And he had a girlfriend. The girlfriend part was only a temporary glitch. Within a week, Devin broke up with Stacey and we became a couple.

Devin was a year older than me, but not more emotionally mature. He was, however, more sexually experienced. His sweet words and tender touch made me feel beautiful and desired. It was addictive ... stronger than any drug I ever tried. I was a virgin, but that changed quickly. I'd do anything to please him. He was my prize. I won Devin fair and square. I easily overlooked his juvenile sense of humor.

The first part of our relationship was mostly spent alone in my townhouse. Mom was usually working or involved in her own social life, so we mostly had the place to ourselves. We watched movies, smoked pot, drank Mad Dog 20/20, talked about mindless things, snuggled, slept, and had sex. A lot of it.

At first, sex was painful. Before long, it started feeling good, really good, and I wanted it as much as he did. But after a few months, his hunger for gratification overpowered mine. If I didn't feel like doing it, Devin pulled out the baby oil and let me know the least I could do was give him a hand job. Feeling like it wasn't okay to say no, I did it.

I swore my undying love to him, but I admit, his childishness started getting on my nerves. He also started drinking more and I didn't care for his drunken personality. He acted like a horny, and equally goofy, twelve-year-old who's never seen a pair of tits before. It wasn't particularly a turn-on.

I barely saw my friends anymore and began feeling suffocated. So, we started hanging out with other people. Our newly formed group spent many nights at the park drinking, smoking pot, dropping acid, or all three. It was almost a contest to see how many foreign substances our bodies could tolerate without dying. We had plenty of great times as a group, but Devin's immaturity became embarrassing.

At fourteen, what your friends think often determines your decisions. No one said anything about Devin to me directly. But I felt they sensed my humiliation. I wanted to move on, but I didn't want to hurt him. I stuck around, even though his drug use increased, and he began acting utterly bizarre.

Then, one day, Devin had an episode at school that changed everything. The combination of drugs he was on is still unclear, but I heard it took three teachers to pry him off the wall. He acted stuck to the hallway lockers like a magnet, yelling out nonsensical statements about things like breakfast cereal, surfboards, and cave paintings. When they managed to get him to the clinic, Devin said someone slipped something into his milk at lunch. No one believed him.

Big George searched Devin's locker. He never busted him and his buddy Tyler after the chasing incident and Devin's current situation gave George great satisfaction. From Devin's locker, he confiscated two hits of LSD, and a Pepsi can fashioned into a bowl with marijuana resin on it.

It was Devin's turn to accompany his parents to Principal Bailey's interrogation room to discuss the aftermath of his misbehavior. Indefinitely suspended from school, his parents checked him into the Pinewood Psychiatric Institute, the local teenage rehabilitation facility. Three times a week, a phone operator patched Devin through, and we had fifteen minutes to talk. I was always cheerful and assured him I would be there when he gets out. No matter how long it takes.

When you're young, two weeks is a long time, a month is forever, and any longer than that is an eternity. I broke my promise. Devin was upset by me leaving something awful, but at the time, I honestly didn't care. *What a bitch I was.* We didn't meet again until several short-lived teenage relationships later.

Gabby dragged me to a party. I was anxious as ever and stood outside while she got us a beer from the keg. I killed it in three gulps. *It was a little cup.* Soon, I chilled out enough to venture inside. We scanned the room for familiar faces. It seemed like all the people Mom had forbidden me to see after my big at-home drug rehabilitation were there. Gabby and I were walking the room and mingling with old friends when I saw him.

Bobbing his head to the music and nursing a bottle of Budweiser, Devin Miller was sitting quietly and alone with his back against the wall, on the living room floor. He was as sexy as ever. I asked to join him. He nodded. We sat there a long time while I talked, and he listened. I felt like I did the first time I saw him. I wanted him, and I would win my prize … again.

I knew I broke his heart and I wanted to make it up to him. I coerced him into talking if I called. I took him on a stroll down memory lane. I reminded him how good sex was and followed it with thoughts of how great it would be now. At the time, I believed sex drove all men. Erotic temptations would catch them, and good head would keep them.

I felt privileged to be welcomed back into Devin's life. I was going to fix the past and heal his heart. I had no idea I was diving into a pool of toxicity.

Chapter 14
Greased with Grime

*T*he events played out over the weekend have my mind spiraling out of sanity. It's Monday morning, and I am physically and mentally wiped the fuck out. Either all the Vicodin I took or my subconscious bubbling to the surface gave me nightmares. I'm more tired after waking up than I was when I went to sleep.

I reach over and open the bottle of Vicodin on my bedside table. Five left. *Holy shit!* Taking fifteen pills in two days undoubtedly explains my drowsiness. I put the bottle in the drawer and promise myself not to take them unless my pain is intolerable … or it's a special occasion.

I don't want to be late to school and deal with Mrs. Schelding's power trip to allow me entry or send me home for a tardy note. I drag my ragged ass out of bed and into the shower.

I sit through my classes in a daze. All I can think about are babies, abuse, lies, and my possible pregnancy. My breasts are swollen and tender like Gabby's, but that's normal for me before I start my period. So, I'm trying not to think about it.

What's killing me is Gabby knowing she's pregnant, but still consuming dangerous substances. I don't get it … she's wanted a baby forever. Her recklessness is disturbing.

I doubt I will ever talk to Gabby about it. It's her body and baby. Besides, I'm clueless on how to approach her. She's grown and should know perfectly well that babies are born in poor health if the mother does exactly what she's doing. When I get pregnant, I will quit everything that can cause harm to my newborn. I don't want to lessen my baby's chance for a full and healthy life before he or she even enters the world. *What the fuck is she thinking?*

I manage to make it through my morning classes, but I don't remember a word said by my teachers. I hope they didn't go over anything on the upcoming test. I may party a lot, but I take school seriously and strive for good grades. Be that as it may, every day I look forward to leaving. Today I'm proud of myself for not skipping out after homeroom.

Five miles past Nate's daycare I remember I'm supposed to pick him up. I turn around. I've been picking him up every Monday for months. I can't believe I forgot. I pull into the parking lot and see Nate standing out front with Mark, the owner of *Kid's Rule Daycare.* I get out of the car and apologize. Mark assures me it's not a big deal. If he wasn't nice about it, I would have broken down in tears, and I don't want

Nate to see that.

I don't get my usual hug, and Nate is oddly quiet the whole ride to the deli. I ask him if he's mad at me for being late. He says no, but I don't fully believe him. He's not acting like himself. Thinking it over, I reckon five-year-olds have bad days too. We pull up to the deli and he hops out. I see Devin through the window working, but don't go in.

I want to crawl into bed and forget the world. But I'm expected at work in thirty minutes. Trying to think positively, I tell myself work will keep my mind off everything buzzing around in my brain.

I get to Med Warehouse at the same time as Penny. I think she purposely schedules us to work together, and that is fine with me. I always look forward to seeing her. She has a calming presence.

"Hiya, pumpkin," Penny says as we walk in the door.

"Hey, Penny, how goes it today?"

"Same ol', same ol'." She notices the bandage around my wrist.

"Oh, hon', what happened?"

"Ah, it's no big deal. Devin and I were wrestling around the other night, and I sprained it."

"Oh, darlin'," she looks at me inquisitively as if she knows I'm lying. "Are you gonna be all right to work?"

"Sure, I'll be fine, no problem, Penny." Moving my facial muscles, I hope for a genuine-looking smile.

I walk to the back room and clock in. Using the stockroom sink, I splash cool water on my face. I take ten deep breaths and count to fifty, then walk to my register. It's a slow day. I ring up toilet paper, wrinkle control cream, cigarettes, and some other boring merchandise.

The store is nearly empty when Justin, the only guy cashier, comes in for his shift. Normally, when work is slow, we chat. He likes to tell me about the sexual adventures he and his older girlfriend have. She's a nymphomaniac, and they fuck anywhere at any time. It's riveting conversation, even if it's not true. But today, I don't feel like hearing it. I straighten the candy and magazine racks by my register repeatedly.

As I rotate the Life-Saver rolls, so all the colors are aligned, Penny walks over and whispers she needs to talk to me. I immediately strain my overheated brain for anything I may have done wrong but can't think of a thing. I turn off my register light and follow Penny down the hair care aisle, and into the back room.

We go into the dismal excuse of an employee's lounge, and I sit down at the rickety table, greased with gunk, grime, and disease.

"Do you want a soda, Rose?"

"Yes please, Pepsi sounds good."

Penny puts change in the machine. "Here ya go sugar-pie."

"Thanks, Penny."

"You betcha." She sits down next to me, hands me my drink, and opens her bottle of spring water.

"Rose, honey, I don't want to pry, but you know you're my favorite. Everyone knows that."

I hadn't known until she just told me, but I am glad

to hear it. Now I'm feeling warm and fuzzy inside.

"Anyway, I can just tell something is wrong with you today. Please tell me if you want me to butt out, honeybun. I promise I won't get my feelins hurt."

"No, Penny, you're fine."

"Okay, well I'm just gonna fire it on out there then."

"Okay, fire away." *Fuck, I'm nervous.*

"Rose, hon', tell me, does that sprained wrist of yours have anything to do with the e.p.t. test you bought Friday? Don't feel you have to answer if you don't want to."

I sit quietly and sip my Pepsi. Keeping my eyes on the table, I feel torn. I want to tell her the truth. Penny reaches her hand out and lays it over mine and rubs my fingers with hers.

"Actually," I say, "I haven't even taken the test yet." I look at her hand on mine. "I've always gotten hurt easily. My wrist is just another stupid accident."

Penny is straining to make an expression that reads belief. She doesn't do a very good job of it. "Well, alright then, sugar, I hope it starts feeling better real soon."

"I'm sure it will." Penny takes her hand off mine.

"Well, if you ever want to talk about anything, please do not hesitate to come to me, okay? In fact, let me give you my home number."

Penny reaches into her smock pocket and pulls out an old receipt. She writes her name and phone number with a smiley face next to it.

"Come on, Rose, we better get back out there before Justin has a meltdown out front all by his lonesome."

Brooks

I walk back to my register and turn the "open" light on. Once the customers taper off, I pull out Penny's phone number and rub the paper between my fingers. I'm more compelled to tell Penny the truth than my mom, or Gabby.

What is it about abuse that causes such embarrassment it has to be kept a secret? Physical or mental, it's a secret trapped inside you like a festering sore ... and you're afraid to tell those who you love the most, those who would protect you.

It's been several years since anyone laid a hand on me in anger.

Chapter 15

Where's the Romance?

*F*rank Warner was the ideal man. He was handsome, educated, wealthy, and from what Mom says, a romantic. Every Saturday, she got a delivery of fresh-cut flowers. The bouquets varied, except for one red rose in the center. Mom cut each stem under cold water and placed it perfectly in the vase. I breathed in the sweet scent and wondered how she knew where each flower belonged.

Mom didn't want help arranging flowers, but she took my advice on what dresses were classy enough to wear at expensive restaurants. I imagined they dined at ballrooms found in storybook illustrations of kings and queens eating sumptuous meals before the royal court. I wasn't invited out to eat, but they brought home leftovers wrapped up in foil shaped like a swan. My taste hadn't bridged beyond the crap kids love, so I didn't get what was so great about the gourmet entrees. But the desserts were delicious!

After dating for two months, Mom and Frank got

married. It was the day after I turned ten. They got married at the courthouse by the Justice of the Peace. *Maybe Frank was saving the "romance" for the honeymoon!*

Anyway, we set up house with Frank in his mini mansion in Maysville Manor. It had four bathrooms, a wraparound porch, and a large backyard with a tire swing hanging from the tallest tree. I spent a lot of afternoons swinging and reading my favorite book, *Super Fudge* by Judy Blume.

Not being on a tight budget, Mom and I went shopping, a lot. I had new clothes for school and more toys and books than I ever dreamed of. Life couldn't be better! Mom and Frank even started taking me to dinner and I brought home foil-sculpted swans too. With my newfound enjoyment of fine dining, a happy meal lost its luster. Sadly, so did Frank.

With Frank's financial help, Mom completed the courses to become a real estate agent. Mom danced into the house belting out Frank Sinatra's "My Way" the day she got her license. Mom always did great at sales, but as her success mounted, Frank's behavior declined. He no longer applauded her or gave her congratulatory gifts. Rather, he became hostile and downright mean.

When Frank was yelling at Mom, I hid under the towels on the bottom of the linen closet. Most of it was muffled, but not all. I heard him tell Mom she was damaged goods, and no one will want her if she leaves him. He told her he picked her up out of the gutter and can put her back there. Frank's words burned into my brain and scarred my soul. I couldn't understand why he was treating Mom that way. She didn't do anything wrong. Regardless, after she succumbed to Frank's tyranny, he started in on me.

When Frank found I wasn't as easy to break with words, he started hitting me instead. Mom used her hands to hold and comfort me. I was so confused. I made sure to be on my best behavior, but I never knew what would set him off. Bent over the bed, my bare ass exposed, he would spank me. The number of strikes depended on my offense. Spilled cereal: two lashes, an unmade bed: three, saying anything construed as disrespectful: too many. I was just a little girl!

I knew it had to be my fault that Mom married Frank. She wanted me to have a loving and stable father figure. Despite my young age, I held incredible guilt for that. I wanted more than anything to be happy again. I wanted to sing and dance and act silly with Mom like we used to.

It was the first day of summer break and Frank wasn't home. Mom and I were so happy to be alone for the day. We made lunch and sat down on the couch to eat and watch our favorite movie, *Grease*. The best part was coming up. Sandy and Danny break into song and dance in the fun house at their school carnival. Mom and I jumped up off the couch, and my plate of chips went flying across the coffee table and onto the floor. We ignored it. We were singing and dancing away. The TV volume was so loud that we didn't hear him come in.

Brooks

Frank stormed in screaming! He told us if we wanted to act like idiots and trash his house like a couple of farm animals then we could, "get the fuck out!" Instead of running to the closet to hide, I jumped between them. Frank raised his hand to Mom, and I screamed for him to hit me instead. When he told me mine was coming, Mom stood there frozen. She acted shocked. Realizing that he was abusing me, she turned a shade of red so deep she looked purple.

Mom demanded I leave the room. I crouched down in the corner instead. I'd never seen her fight back before. I watched everything that wasn't nailed down get picked up and go flying out of Mom's hands. Vases, picture frames, books, candle holders, the radio, and everything else Mom could lift became projectile missiles programmed to detonate upon contact with Frank. When she noticed me in the corner, she ordered me to get what I couldn't live without because "we're getting the hell out of here!"

I was scared, but when Mom said we were leaving, my fear turned into excitement. I ran to my bedroom and danced while packing my Strawberry Shortcake book bag with a couple of outfits, stuffed animals, books, a pair of shoes, and my Winnie the Pooh Pez dispenser. When I returned to the living room, the hurricane of household items had ceased. I didn't see Frank or Mom and I got nervous. My chest tightened up and my heart was racing.

Mom surely wouldn't have left without me. I nervously peeked out of the front window. I saw Frank on the

81

street talking to our neighbor. His nose was bloody, his shirt was torn, and he had a cut over his left eye. I smiled. I saw Mom slumped against her car smoking a cigarette. I started running toward her, and she hollered for me to get her purse and keys. I rushed back into the house, grabbed her stuff, and the *Grease* video out of the VCR.

As we sped off, I heard Frank yell, "you better never come back, you stupid bitch!" *Thank you, dear Lord, I owe you one!*

Chapter 16
Twisted Nipples

Parked on the street in front of his house, I'm waiting for Devin's black Dodge Charger to come barreling around the bend. It's Friday, one week from the night Devin fractured my wrist. We agreed to take the pregnancy test tonight. I've been here for an hour. Anticipating his reaction to the test results is exhausting! I want rainbows and sunshine, but realistically, it'll probably be dirt and dead flowers. I'm driving myself crazy with possibilities. And my pack of cigarettes is almost empty.

Trying to determine if I'm pregnant without taking a test, I'm kneading my breasts and pinching my nipples to gauge their sensitivity. They are swollen and tender. More than ever before. I see what Gabby meant when she told me her nipples hurt if you blew on them. Even though I'm becoming increasingly sore with each twist of my fingers, I can't stop! I question the validity of my senses. Is the tenderness real, or have I lodged the idea so deep within my psyche that it's my subconscious creating the pain and not my nerve endings?

Devin was sweet to me on the phone earlier. He gave no indication of hesitation. I'll wait fifteen more minutes. I need to give my nipples a rest. I take the directions out of the e.p.t. box and read them repeatedly. I try to read the Spanish version and imagine if anyone is listening, they'd be embarrassed for me. I chuckle, it reminds me of my old friend, Gina. We'd walk to the corner store and speak to each other in a spontaneously made-up language. We thought we were so clever and knew for sure that everyone who heard us would think we were from an exotic land - one mysterious and intriguing. Now I know they were probably just holding their laughter until we left.

Fifteen minutes have long passed. I start my car and leave to go buy cigarettes. In the convenience store, I grab a cold Pepsi from the cooler and a pack of smokes off the rack. The clerk is jabbing her jaws on the phone and doesn't acknowledge my presence by making eye contact or a quick gesture. Poor customer service is one of my pet peeves. If you don't like people, don't get a job working with them. It's that simple.

I've been waiting almost ten minutes for this rude-ass cashier to end her call. My heavy sighs, toe-tapping, and fingernails clicking on the countertop are ignored. She's trying to convince someone that her check is in the mail. I am beyond agitated. Still not having acknowledged my existence, she ends her conversation with, "screw you mister, you worthless bull-headed horse's ass!" She slams the phone down onto its cradle and bubbles rise from the bottom of my Pepsi bottle.

"Sorry about that," she says. "Those damn bill collectors just don't back off. I paid the bill for Christ's sake!"

I want to rip the phone out of the wall and wrap the cord around her neck until she can't speak anymore, but I look at her and nod like I can relate to her troubles. My agitation isn't worth the confrontation. Ringing me up, she continues to ramble on about "jerk-off" bill collectors. I imagine her slipping on the spilled cherry slushy behind the counter rendering her unconscious, and I crack a little smile. Back in my car, I light a cigarette, close my eyes, and breathe deep to the count of ten.

Driving back to Devin's house, I can't decide if I should be mad or concerned. Although anger is easier for me to contend with, I've dealt with it too much lately, so I decide to be concerned. Before I went to the store, I did everything I could think of, short of masturbation, to pass the time. Now that I'm back at his house and Devin still isn't home, I really am worried. I gather myself and walk to the front door. I hope his parents know where he is.

Right before my finger hits the doorbell, Devin pulls up. I'm relieved. But then, I hear the car door slam.

Chapter 17
Seeing Double

*F*rom the porch, I hear Devin cursing under his breath while I watch him stomp up the driveway. When we spoke earlier, he was fine. He even made me feel at ease. I want to know why he's late, but I'll most likely get blasted if I ask. *What's new?* I put it to the test.

"Are you okay? I was getting worried. I've been waiting for over an hour."

"Yeah, Rose, I'm fine. I know I'm late; you don't have to tell me."

"I'm sorry, Devin. I was worried, that's all."

"It's only been an hour, for fuck's sake … my tire blew. I had to get a tow and buy a new one. So, I'm sorry for messing up your precious time schedule, Rose. Jesus Christ!"

I follow Devin up the stairs and into his bedroom without so much as a murmur.

Thoughts of Mom's ex-husband infiltrate my brain. Frank treated Mom how Devin is treating me … like shit. And she didn't do anything to deserve it either. Living through Mom's marriage was a nightmare. *How could I let myself fall into the same trap?*

In the beginning, I stayed with Devin to make up for ditching him years ago. I thought I could heal his heart by being everything he needed me to be. And more. I never even turned down a request for a blow job. And I truly thought having a baby would make things better. You know, to bring us closer together.

To maintain self-transparency, I wouldn't have missed a full week of birth control pills if I didn't want to get pregnant. But after Devin broke my wrist, from merely mentioning the possibility, I'm terrified of what he may do if the result is positive. He promised that he'd never hurt me again, but I don't trust him. *This fearing-my-boyfriend shit needs to end.*

Devin stands stoic by the door. I sit quietly waiting for him to speak. Suddenly, he snaps, "do you have the test?"

I jump. "Yes, I brought it." I look at the bag that's been hiding under the seat in my car for a week. It still has Mom's candy in it.

"Well, are you gonna take it or what?" Devin isn't calming down.

"Yes, of course. You want me to do it right now?"

He reaches into his pocket, "Fuck!"

Oh, Jesus, what now?

"I forgot to get more smokes," he snarls, "and I was just at the gas station. God Damn it!"

Before going down the stairs, he turns in a huff. "Go

ahead and piss on the stick, and we'll look at it when I get back."

As soon as he leaves, I take the test, set it on the bathroom counter, and note the time. Five minutes ... my fate. I'm glad he had to leave. If it's positive, I have time to prepare for his reaction. I light a cigarette, apologize to my potential embryo, and take another drag.

I've studied every inch of Devin's room, looked at the bruising on my wrist, sat here in a cloud of disgust and raging anxiety, and power smoked three cigarettes. It's been seven minutes. Having read the instructions repeatedly, I know two blue lines mean I'm pregnant. I look at the test from outside the bathroom door. I'm seeing double.

I hear the clanging of keys hit the metal dish by the front door. My hands get shakier with every squeaky step up the stairs. I say a prayer. *I'm not sure if God hears me.*

Devin opens the bedroom door and sees me trembling on his bed. He goes into the bathroom and two seconds later, the pregnancy test stick flies out of the bathroom door and hits the wall beside my head.

"Oh, my fucking God, Rose! This can't be happening!"

I grab a pillow and hold it tight.

"You know what?" he continues. "I don't believe you. I think you're full of shit, Rose. How do I even know it's mine?"

"I'm not a slut, Devin. And you fucking know it! It's your baby. Why do you even say shit like that? I've never been unfaithful to you." I try to take a deep breath but can't. "I thought you'd be happy."

"You thought I'd be happy?" He laughs. "Well, that's just great, Rose. Why the hell would you think that?"

"Because you'll be a great dad," I whisper. *Denial is currently my saving grace.*

"Oh please, Rose, I don't want to hear that shit. I can't handle this! Not now, not again!"

My body is on fire. "What do you mean you can't handle this again?"

"You need to get an abortion, Rose. I'll pay for half."

"You didn't answer me, Devin."

"I meant what I said. You need to have an abortion."

"But I thought you loved me. I'll be a great mom, I promise." *What is my problem?*

Devin punches the wall next to the bathroom door and splits the brown paneling. "Stop with the mom and dad bullshit, Rose. How many times do I need to say it?"

"Just fucking tell me, Devin, what exactly can you not go through again?"

"I'm talking about Nate, Rose. Okay? Nate."

"What about Nate? I don't understand."

"Of course, you don't."

"Okay, well help me understand, then!" *This is fucking torture.*

"Nate is my son."

"What?" I question my hearing. "Nate is what?" The room starts to spin.

"Nate is my son from my ex-girlfriend ... you know,

Stacey." He clears his throat. "We were fourteen and her parents were forcing her to put the baby up for adoption. My parents agreed to raise him so he could stay with family."

I barely make it to the toilet before throwing up. On the cold bathroom floor, emotionally terrorized and fueled by anger, I punch myself in the stomach. Devin stands watching and does nothing. Momentarily detached from reality, I continue to hit myself until my mind suddenly clears. *What am I doing? I'll never forgive myself if I hurt my baby.*

"Okay, Devin, so tell me if I've got this right?" I sputter through staggered breathing. "You had a kid with Stacey and kept him, but now I'm pregnant and you're screaming at me to get an abortion? Did you love her? Do you not love me?"

"Yes, Rose, I loved her."

"What about me?"

"Yes, I love you too."

"Then, what the hell?"

"I love you, Rose ... but not enough."

Silence to the count of ten deaths.

"I'm sorry, what? Not enough?" I kick the bathroom door shut and call for the reaper. I thought I prepared for the worst, but I didn't. This is a slit-your-wrist level of pain.

I don't know how much time passes before I pick myself up off the bathroom floor. Doesn't matter, it was long enough for me to decide I'm done. I pick up my purse and stand in front of the bedroom door. There are so many spiteful things I want to say, so many insults I want to spit, and so many feelings I want to unleash on this son of a bitch.

"I'm done for good, Devin. I can't take it anymore. I thought I could, but I was wrong. Why did you even leave Stacey in the first place? You know, since you loved her so much?" *I fucking hate him.* "Actually, I don't wanna know. Have fun watching your parents raise your brother-son." I turn around and grab the handle to open the door and flash back to one week ago, the night he broke my wrist. It gives me a reason to not look back.

Devin follows me outside and as I get into my car, he spews out, "you're gonna have an abortion, Rose, right?"

Chapter 18
Scream Until It Hurts

I cut my eyes back at Devin and holler, "Go fuck yourself!" I don't care who hears me, so long as he does. I can't get out of his neighborhood fast enough. I never want to see his face or that house again. Down past the church with the broken stained-glass windows, I start to hyperventilate and pull off the road. I turn my radio up to max volume and scream as loud as I can until my throat hurts.

I hear a loud crash … thunder. The light of day has dulled, and it starts pouring rain. I turn on the headlights and windshield wipers, but I can barely see out of my glazed eyes. Gabby's house is only five minutes away. I can do this. *Just breathe and focus, Rose … breathe and focus.*

I park on the street in front of her house. Looking in the visor mirror, I see my face is painted with purple eye shadow, pink blush, and black mascara. It looks like one big bruise. I take a tissue from the glove compartment and try to fix it, but it's only making it worse. I punch the steering wheel, shut off the engine, and step out into the cold rain.

Gabby answers the door. "Oh, my God, Rose. What happened? I'll kill that motherfucker!"

"Gabby, I'm pregnant."

"What?" She wraps her arm around my shoulder and guides me out of the rain, through the front door, and into her bedroom.

"Not enough, Gabby ... not enough." I fall onto her bed.

"Not enough what, Rose? What's happening?"

I bury my head in a pillow. "He loves me, but not enough. Devin told me to get an abortion ... he'll pay half."

"Oh my God, he said that? That is so fucked! I'm sorry, my sweet Rose." Gabby lies on the bed beside me.

"I can't believe this, Gabby, I'm fucking crushed!"

"He's a dead man!" Gabby is fired up.

"No, no, hold on, it gets better. Nate, Devin's little brother, is actually his son. His fucking son, Gabby!"
"Hold up! What?"

I move the pillow from my face and look into her eyes. "Devin's parents adopted Nate when his girlfriend, Stacey, was forced to give him up five years ago. He loved her enough, but not me. What the fuck did I do wrong? I've been nothing but good to him."

"You didn't do anything wrong. Devin is an asshole. I mean, come on Rose, he's been treating you shitty for a long time. Fuck that loser! You're better off without him!"

"But Gabby, I'm pregnant with his ... unwanted child."

"Unwanted?" Gabby looks at me, squints her eyes and scowls. "What are you talking about, Rose? You want the baby, don't you?"

For years, Gabby and I have dreamed about being pregnant at the same time and raising our kids together. "Of course, I want the baby! I got pregnant on purpose, Gabbs. I didn't take my pills. I thought a baby would make everything better. I couldn't have been more wrong! I'm such an idiot!"

She takes a minute to let that sink in. "No, Rose. You're not an idiot. You just wanted the same thing as me ... a gentle soul that will love you as much as you love them. You don't need Devin to have your baby. I will be here for you, always. Fuck him! We got this, girl!"

"You promise?" I sniffle. "It hurts so bad, Gabby."

"It's gonna be okay, sweet Rose. I promise you, it will."

Gabby strokes my hair and starts singing *Kumbaya*. She knows Mom sang that to me when I was a little girl while she rubbed my back to help me fall asleep. Gabby can't sing worth a shit, but it's super sweet of her to try.

"Can I crash here with you tonight, Gabbs?"

"Yes, of course you can." She smiles, "you better go call your mom."

In the kitchen, I lean against the counter and steady my breathing by slowly counting backwards from fifty to one. It's vital I get through this conversation without letting on that I'm an emotional wreck. I try to trick my brain by smiling, clear my throat, pick up the phone, and dial.

Mom answers. "Hello."

"Hey, Mom, it's me."

"Well, hey there, sweetheart. What are you up to?" Mom always sounds chipper and sweet; I don't know how she does it.

"I'm at Gabby's. She had a tough day and asked me to come over." *Hell, what's another lie or two?*

"Is she gonna be okay?" Mom cares as much about Gabby as I do.

Keeping my facial façade in play, I respond, "yes, she just had a disagreement with her boyfriend and doesn't want to be alone. I'm gonna stay overnight."

"You and Gabby are lucky to have each other. See you in the morning?"

"No, I have to work, but I'm off at two."

"Well, I won't be far behind you, then. Give Gabby a hug for me." *It's almost over.*

"Okay, Mom, will do. Love you." *I think this pretend smiling actually works.*

"I love you too, sweetheart."

"See you tomorrow." *A few silent tears, but no sniffles or crackling voice … mission accomplished.*

I find Gabby sitting on the living room floor. *The Jetsons* is playing on the TV. I can't help but to smile. It was my favorite cartoon. I was so excited for the year 2000 when we can pop a tiny bean in the microwave and a hiccup later, a five-course meal pops out. I sit down next to Gabby and lay my head on her shoulder. Again, she assures me everything is gonna be all right. I want to believe her.

"Well, Rose, we'd better get used to watching kid's shows and cartoons." Gabby starts to giggle. "Holy shit, I must've seen *Little Mermaid* a thousand times."

I'm perplexed. She's excited about a childhood memory. I didn't think that'd be possible, but her happy energy is infectious and I'm starting to feel more relaxed.

"So, Gabbs, have you been thinking about baby names?"

Without hesitation. "Cameron Luke, and Cassandra Lynn. You?"

"Abigail Rose, and Austin Wade."

We talk about things like how we'll dress our kids in matching outfits, take them to the park, and teach them about animals at the zoo. We speculate on how much our bodies are going to change. We both hope we won't get stretch marks. I hope my boobs won't sag and Gabby hopes hers will get bigger.

"So, Rose, are your boobs swollen and sensitive too?"

"Yes, oh my God, are they ever!"

Gabby leans toward me and pinches my nipple.

"Ouch! You bitch!" I swat her hand and pinch the hell out of her nipple too.

"Ouch, Rose! What the fuck?"

"You did it to me first!"

We spend the next few minutes competing in our newly invented sport of nipple pinching. The pain and laughter distract my mind from the negative bullshit eating me alive.

The doorbell rings. We both wave our white flags, and the event is deemed over. Gabby gets up to answer the door and I hear her yelling. *What the fuck?* I jump up and peek around the foyer wall. It's Devin. I don't think he saw me. I crawl down the hallway to Gabby's bedroom and cover my ears with my hands. The yelling is muffled like it was when I was hiding in the linen closet as a kid. I can't make out everything, but I do hear the word, "police" and the door slam.

Gabby finds me on the floor, next to her bed, rocking myself back and forth. "Don't worry, Rose, he won't be coming back." *Gabby's taking care of me like I've taken care of her.*

"He's lucky I didn't kill him." Gabby's face is hot lava red. "Let's go out back and get some fresh air. I'm burning up ... I need a smoke."

Gabby extends her arm and I take her hand. She helps me to my feet, and I follow her out the back door. I take the cigarette she offers me but feel guilty for smoking before I even light it. I tell her my head hurts, it will only make it worse, and give it back.

"Gabbs, I'm exhausted. I need to work in the morning and I'm ready to close my eyes."

Gabby taps her cigarette out on the bottom of her shoe and flicks it onto the lawn. "Come on, sweets, let's get you set up."

"Can I wear that huge purple nightshirt of yours ... the one I frequently try to steal?"

"You bet. Can I do anything else for you? Are you thirsty? Hungry? Anything?"

"You're so good to me, Gabbs, thank you. All I need is sleep."

I change into Gabby's nightshirt and tuck myself into bed. She has the softest sheets I've ever felt. As soon as my head hits the pillow, my mind goes blank.

Chapter 19
Concrete Collision

I forgot to set Gabby's alarm clock. I wake up with less than an hour to be at work, and I have a raging headache. I consider calling out sick. Recently, I questioned myself as to if I was responsible or not. I didn't come up with a concise answer. Now, I have no choice. I need to be accountable. Devin's not going to help. *Fuck him!* And I am not getting an abortion!

I wash a few aspirin down with a glass of grape juice and do my best to look presentable. I borrow a pair of Gabby's jeans, but I have to wear yesterday's shirt. Hers are tiny. I hope no one notices the soda stain from where I missed my mouth last night.

Ten minutes late, I walk through the entrance of Med Warehouse. On the drive here, Devin's words played in my head … *not enough, Not Enough, NOT ENOUGH.* How I'm functioning somewhat normally is a mystery. Strategically walking through the store, I manage to avoid eye contact with shoppers and luckily no one stops me to ask questions. I have a problem with emotions. Even when I try to mask them, they read plainly. *And I don't like explaining myself to strangers.*

And I also don't want to chat with Penny. *She sees me.*

"Well, hey there, gal! How ya doin'? Did you have yourself a good weekend?" Penny asks while she's filling in the empty squares on the scheduling sheet. I don't respond, and she looks up at me. "Oh, sugar, what's goin' on? You got me concerned, hon', oh, yes you do … talk to me, pumpkin' … what's happening? What can I do?"

The look of vulnerability in Penny's eyes draws me to her. *Maybe I can confide in her.*

"Penny, remember when you told me I could talk to you if I ever wanted?"

"Yes, love, of course I do." Penny opens her arms and walks toward me. I trip over my feet and fall into a hug with her.

"I need to talk."

I feel Penny nodding her head, and she tells me to follow her. We walk through the back room to the outside exit. She turns off the alarm, and we step out into the sunshine. The warmth feels good on my face and dries the tears on my cheeks.

"My wrist … Devin did it."

No warning, I opened my mouth and the truth just spilled out.

"You're so brave, Rose. It's never easy to talk about abuse. Especially when you're the victim. I know, sweetheart, I know … all too well. Thank you for trusting me."

Immediately, I know I made the right decision. Penny hands me a tissue from her smock pocket.

"When Devin found out I may be pregnant, he started yelling and calling me names. He even accused me of cheating. I tried to leave, Penny, but he twisted my wrist and yanked it off the doorknob ... it's broken."

"Oh, you sweet thing, I'm so sorry. It's not your fault. You need to know that straight away, hon'... it is not your fault." Penny's voice is firm but medicinal.

"But I feel like it's my fault ..."

"No, Rose, it's never okay for anyone to put their hands on you. Ya did nothin' to deserve that treatment and ya can't allow it to keep on goin' ... I won't let ya."

"I'm sorry, Penny." *I feel like I let her down.*

"No, sweetie don't be sorry. Ya did the right thing, I promise. You are not alone hon'. I'm here whenever ya need me."

Penny sounds genuine. But why does she care so much? I know we get along and have fun working together, and she did say I was her favorite. I don't want to be a bother but I have no one else I trust to tell the truth.

"Rose, look at me, sugar." Penny pulls me out of my thoughts. "I'd like to share my story, if you're up for hearin' it?"

"Of course, Penny. You're helping me so much right now. I thought I was gonna burden myself with this secret for the rest of my life."

Penny tells me to sit on the wooden bench by the picnic table while she goes in to make sure everything's under control. The area outside is surrounded by overgrown shrubbery and wildflowers blooming in every color. Aside from the bees, it's a nice little spot for quiet repose.

While I wait, it occurs to me that the name I chose for a baby girl, Abigail, is the name of the first Cabbage Patch Kid I had. She was the prettiest doll with blond hair and green eyes. It speaks to how young I am to be having a baby when my only reference to names are those of toy dolls.

Penny walks around the side of the building with two bottles of water. She hands me one. "Ya holdin' up alright, darlin'?"

"I am." The cold water feels good going down my throat.

Penny uses her hand to shade her face from the sun. "Four years ago, after my marriage ended, I moved here from my hometown in Kennesaw, Georgia." Penny inhales deeply. I count to twelve before she exhales. "I needed to make a fresh start, ya see."

She tilts her head back and lets the sun glow on her face. She has the longest, most pretty, strawberry-blond eyelashes.

"Me and my ex-husband was fightin' … it was always somethin' with Brighton. He won't never happy. I was blamed for whatever was wrong with him, and he liked to slap me around. Especially, when he was drinkin' … and he was always drinkin'."

I see the water bottle in her hand is shaking. She removes the cap and takes three big swallows.

"Anyhow, this one day was super awful. And as it turned out, it was the worst day of my life."

I'm starting to understand Penny's concern for me.

"Brighton was on a four-day bender and had already blackened my eye and busted my nose. Now he was yellin' at me 'bout where I put his dang car keys. I didn't put em' anywhere. I wanted him to leave me alone … I sure as hell won't hidin' his keys from him. But there was no stoppin' once he got to goin'."

Penny finishes her bottle of water and continues, "I was bent over the sink tryin' to stop my nose from bleedin' when I heard poundin' on the front door. It had to been hard poundin' to hear it over Brighton's yellin'. I was hopin' it was the police, but I won't that lucky."

I would never have imagined Penny had gone through anything like this.

"Next thing I knew," she continues, "I was hearin' my brother's voice. I could hear Henry and Brighton yellin' at each other. I stuck toilet paper up my nose and ran to the livin' room. My brother seen my black eye and bloody nose, and he just flat out lost his mind. They got to pushin' each other and ended up out there on the balcony. I lived up high on the fourth floor. I was scared almost to death."

I want to kill this Brighton bastard.

"Rose, I watched my brother, dear sweet Henry, go over the top of the railing. I heard him hit the concrete. I knew he was dead. I wished I was dead too." She wipes her tears away, clasps her hands together, and raises them to her chin. *I think she's praying.*

"Oh my God, Penny." *I'm not sure what to say.* "How do you recover from something so horrific?"

"Well, darlin', it took time ... a long time. Brighton will spend the rest of his days in prison, but I don't care 'bout him no more."

She pauses to rub her eyes.

"I'm gonna see my brother again in Heaven one day ... and knowing that gives me courage to continue on when I need it. Henry was a good man. Since my folks were killed in a car accident when we were kids, all we had was each other. He was my best friend. I miss him every day."

"So that's how you ended up here?"

"Yep, darlin', this place is where I picked my fresh start to be. I pulled my map out, closed my eyes, and put my finger on it. I kinda think God put me in this town just for you."

"I think you may be right."

"Promise me something, Rose."

"Anything."

"Don't let yourself get stuck like I did. You get on outta there fast as ya can and don't look back!" Penny puts her hand on mine and squeezes, "I mean it, Rose. You deserve happiness and to be treated like a queen. Run fast and far ... even if ya are pregnant. Ya hear me, sugar? You go on and take your fresh start right now."

"I can't thank you enough, Penny. Yes, I promise."

Chapter 20
A Rum Reaction

The weight of Devin's abuse has lifted from the center of my frontal lobe, and I'm able to focus on what matters most, the baby brewing in my belly. I will never fall into another abusive relationship. And I don't need Devin in my life to have my baby. Mom raised me on her own. And I turned out … to be a drug-using pothead and pregnant at eighteen. Hold on, let me rethink that. Whatever, the important thing is that, with Mom's support, everything will be okay. I just need to get it.

On the calendar, I see she's off early. Perfect. I've got time to figure out how to tell her, but not too much time to chicken out.

I try to memorize my thoughts … unsuccessfully. It was foolish to think I could rehearse this conversation. Predicting Mom's response is also proving to be a challenge. Oh God, here she is. I'm not ready. My heart is in my throat.

"Rose, honey, I'm home. I picked up some dinner.

Where are you?"

I walk to the kitchen and see Mom unloading a bag of KFC.

"Hey, Mom. Chicken … awesome, I'm starved." I grab two paper plates and fix us both a soda with ice. I can't stop smiling no matter how hard I try. And Mom knows me too well. When I'm looking super happy for no given reason, she thinks I'm up to something … of course, she's usually right.

"You're looking cheery, Rose. That's always nice to see. What's going on in your world?"

How do I say this? I know, I won't … I'll write it.

With a shaky hand and a clever thought, I jot down a message in our notebook. "Your feet stink, and you don't love Jesus!" Mom used to tease me with that taunt … it always made her laugh.

Below my attempt to put her in a happy place, I write, "I'm pregnant, Mom. Love you!" I draw a heart beside it, take a deep breath and exhale as I slide it across the table. She looks down at the paper and back up, twice. The first time she smiled … not the second. I figured she wouldn't be thrilled about it, but I didn't anticipate the furrowed brow and pouty face.

"Seriously, Rose?" Mom drops her head and closes her eyes.

"Yeah, Mom. Seriously." Negative thoughts come crashing down. Damn me!

She opens her eyes but doesn't look at me. "Well, I certainly wasn't expecting this. I'm not sure what to say, Rose." She sighs heavily and continues to stare at the wall.

Beads of sweat start dripping down the sides of my face and the back of my neck. I don't know what to think. I've never known Mom to be this rigid. Her silence is scaring me. My heart is racing, and my body feels heavy. I'm struggling for strength while holding back tears.

"Have you thought about what you're going to do?"

"What do you mean?"

"Well, the way I see it, you have two options—abortion or adoption. How does Devin feel?"

I gasp for air; I can't believe she just said that. "Devin told me to get an abortion, and he'll pay for half of it. I never want to see him again." I push my plate of chicken away and cross my arms. "He got mad, Mom. Are you mad at me too?"

Mom was supposed to be supportive from the get-go, but she can't even look at me. It's hard to breathe as I sit here waiting for what she'll say next.

"No, dear, I'm not mad, just surprised and a little in shock. How did this happen? You are on birth control, right?" She looks like she's holding in gas.

I just got sucker-punched by my mom. To me, her response isn't terribly different from Devin's. I was counting on her comfort and support. I can't get an abortion, and I can't give my baby away. *And since when is Mom not all accepting, loving, and supportive?*

"When Devin told me to get an abortion, Mom, it was hurtful, but not as much as his reason." I take a napkin and dry my tears. "He told me that he loves me, but 'not enough' ... I thought I was going to die right there."

"Oh, dear, that's awful. I'm so sorry, sweetheart." *Finally, she looks me in my eyes.*

"Yeah, well it gets even better, Mom. He's already got a kid."

"What?"

"Nate ... Nate is his son from the girl he was with before me. Devin loved her enough to have a baby."

"Nate is Devin's son? Whoa, hold on." Mom stands up, gets the Rum from the freezer, and pours it in her Coke. "When did you find out?"

"Last night."

"Why didn't you come home? Why did you go to Gabby's?"

"Because I was so broken up. I didn't want you to see me. And, honestly, I wasn't ready to tell you."

"Okay." She pauses. "This is a lot, Rose."

"I know, Mom, I'm sorry. But I can't have an abortion. I can't get rid of my baby like that."

"Well then, have you thought about adoption?"

"I can't do that either, Mom." My heart is beating to a dueling drum line. "I can't give my baby away. That's abandonment. I can't be like Gabby's mom ... or my dad."

"Oh boy." She stands, not looking at me ... again. "I need to use the bathroom. I'll be right back."

Silence ... everywhere but in my head. I thought I'd feel relieved after telling her, but I'm more nervous than ever. It's not like Mom to hesitate when I really need her ... I never even considered that. Would she really not help me?

When Mom comes back into the room, I can tell she was crying. I don't want to upset her further, but I need to know.

"Mom, why didn't you give me another option? You know, the one where you tell me you will help and everything's gonna be okay?"

"Oh, sweetheart ... honestly, I'm at a point in my life where I don't want to raise another baby."

"You won't be raising a baby ... I will!"

"I know that's what you want to believe, honey, but the brunt of the responsibility will fall on me. For instance, how do you think you will afford to raise the baby? What will you do when he or she needs you, but you have to be in class ... because you will be going to college. What about then? I don't want you, or me, to be bogged down with a baby. I want you to get your education and to live a good life."

I have no words, only disappointment.

"Rose, I'm sorry I'm not saying what you want to hear." Mom picks up the pen and starts doodling on a page in the notebook. She's nervous.

"I thought you'd offer to help right from the start, Mom."

She looks at me and I see her emotions evolving. First, she looked stern and angry, now she looks softer and more empathetic.

"Mom, I can still get an education and live a good life with a baby. You know I can do anything I put my mind to ... you're the one who drilled that in my head."

"Oh, Rose, Rose, Rose ..."

"Mom ... yes, yes, yes?"

"Okay."

"Okay, what?" *Oh please, dear Lord, let her be having a change of heart.*

"You need to make me some promises if I'm going to help."

"Of course, Mom, anything ... what?" *I'm making a lot of promises lately. I need to promise myself to keep them.*

"You will go on to further your education so you can support your child when you're no longer living with me. And you will never give up on chasing your dreams, no matter what."

"Done." *I am so relieved.* "Thank you, Mom, I won't let you down."

She raises her eyebrows and lowers her chin. "You'd better not."

Mom slides my plastic fork and plate of chicken back in front of me. Finally, she's smiling.

"Holy crap," she giggles, "I'm gonna be a grandma."

"I didn't think about that, Granny!"

"Oh, Rose, you stop right now!"

"Why, Granny?"

"Rose."

"Okay, fine."

"Thank you."

I figure now is a good a time to fill her in on Gabby's big news too.

"By the way, Mom, guess what?"

"Oh no, there's something else? Are you trying to kill me?" She puts her hands together like she's praying.

"Gabby's pregnant too."

"No, you're kidding, right?" Mom shakes her head and grins. "And I thought you two were already a handful. Lord, help us all!"

We laugh.

"Hey, Mom."

"Yes, Rose."

"I love you!"

Mom takes our notebook, writes something, and slides it across the table to me.

"I love you too, Rose. Everything will be okay."

Yes, exactly what I needed to know.

Chapter 21
Lucy, The Great

Several heart-wrenching days have passed since I last visited my diary. Normally, I'd sit on the side of my bathtub, with candles lit, the fan on, and the window open, smoking weed while I write. Now that I'm pregnant, I need to get used to doing shit without a buzz.

In my bedroom closet, I retrieve "Lucy" from the inside pocket of my raincoat. Naming a diary can't be that unusual. People give names to other inanimate objects, like cars and boats. Naming a boat, however, makes more sense to me than a car. After all, if a boat doesn't have a name, it'll surely sink. Say what you will, that's what I choose to believe.

Anyway, Lucy is the only secret keeper I can confide in, honestly and openly, no matter the subject, without judgement, repercussions, regrets, or rebuttals.

I fill my vintage Strawberry Shortcake glass with orange juice and add a couple ice cubes to lessen the acidity... it burns my tongue. I toss the seven extra pillows off the couch—Mom has a thing for pillows—and wrap myself up with my Vincent van Gogh blanket. I set my glass of juice on the wooden coaster on the coffee table, snuggle into the corner of the couch, and write:

Dear Lucy,

My, oh my, oh my... It has been a hell of a week. Shit I never fathomed has happened and I'm thankful to come out alive. I can't say unscathed, but I'm not dead, so that's good. I can't regurgitate all that's happened ... or risk carpal tunnel. So, I'll be brief:

DEVIN: I never knew a pain so malicious existed. I do NOT need him in my life, and I will take every measure to be sure that's how it stays. It hurts that he doesn't want the baby ... or me, but it also makes it easier to paint him out of the picture. I'm not sure how long it's gonna take to recover from his abuse. From what Penny said, it will be a while. I guess I'll find out.

NATE: Wow, that beautiful little kid has somehow turned into a mirage of an elaborate prank. I can't even begin to deal with it.

GABBY: I don't know what that girl is thinking. She's always been immature, but she's also 18 with a baby on the way. It's time she gets her shit together and grows up. I'm disappointed in her smoking and drinking and dropping out of school, and that makes me sad. Hopefully, she'll come to her senses and quit. Maybe I'll figure out how to talk to her about it ... if something happens and she loses this baby, she'll never recover. She did, however, take care of me when I needed her most ... just like all the times I've taken care of her, and that makes me happy.

PENNY: I never realized just how integral she'd be in my life. She's sweet, caring, and trustworthy. She's lived through much worse than I ever have. And I refuse to let myself get into such a situation as hers. I credit her for breaking me of abusive relationships. I'm determined to take my fresh start right now. Thank you, my dear, Penny.

MOM: I was hurt when she suggested abortion or adoption. After our talk, I understand where she was coming from when she expressed not wanting to raise another child. It's a huge burden to put on her and I recognize that now. I couldn't be more thankful or feel more blessed by her change of heart and agreement to help me. Plain and simple, I'd be lost without her.

My strength has been tested, my faith has been questioned, and my heart has been broken.

I've been scorched by the truth. And I've burned others with deceit. But I don't deserve the scars that have been heaved back at me.

My reality has been turned upside down, and my mind has been turned inside out.

I've been abused with words, broken by actions

(literally), and crippled by rejection.

I've lived in fear and denial. I've been stunned, shocked, and let down … and I've been picked back up.

I've been forced to grow up and counseled not to give up.

I'm hateful and grateful.

I have a baby in my belly and Mom by my side.

I have escaped the abuse and been rescued by those who live true in my heart. The road ahead won't be easy, but it will be guided by love. Love for my family, love for my friends … and love for myself.

Until next time, peace out,

Rose Riley Moon

Chapter 22
Getting Laid in the Shade

*T*oday, I'm being freed from the chains of high school to take my turn in the world beyond, or so Principal Bailey will proclaim. You go, Class of 1992. I've been looking forward to this for four long years. Behind the blue curtain on the stage in the auditorium, while waiting for the ceremony to begin, students are reminiscing, laughing, crying, hugging, and autographing yearbooks.

Frankly, I couldn't care less about memorializing my high school connections. All my real friends are older and have already graduated or dropped out like Gabby did. Having bullshit sentiments from strangers in a picture book won't make my future brighter but I play along and exchange my yearbook with whoever hands me theirs … it's the nice thing to do. Seriously, I'm sort of thrilled to participate in this antiquated ritual. I write the same thing in everyone's *Memoria Libri*:

"All dreams can come true if you have the
courage to chase them."
— Rose Moon

Seeing as my classmates know me as little as I know them, I'm curious to see what they write. Flipping through the pages, I come across a lot of generic shit like, "stay cool," "keep partying," and "I wish I got to know you better." But as I go along, the messages get much deeper. On page 77, next to the picture of the wrestling team, a wise senior writes, "have fun in the sun and get laid in the shade." And my two favorites, "to a cute girl with big boobs" and "I never told you, but I think you have a great ass." *How thoughtful.*

Boy, I'm cranky. It must be my baby-toting hormones, with a side of disdain for the white graduation gown I'm wearing. Our school colors are blue and gold ... why the fuck do we have to wear white? *Who dropped that ball?* Wearing white boosts my cup size to an F, and I look like I'm wearing a pitched satin tent. I hate it! I wanted to pick up my diploma from the school office and be done with it, but Mom insisted I attend the ceremony. It's the least I can do.

Mr. Cook, the science teacher with Grateful Dead stickers on his door and a cocaine habit, gathers the students and reminds us of what to do. First, we line up in alphabetical order by last names, then slowly follow along to our seats in the front three rows. I'm sitting next to Ross Morton. We were friends our freshman year but soon blended with two very different cliques. He became a geeky nerd, and I became a pothead. Oddly enough, we sit shoulder to shoulder sporting gold sashes. I heard Ross whisper to his girlfriend that it's not fair. Maybe not, but it's also not my fault that the school's curriculum consisted mostly of mindless busy-work assigned by less than motivated teachers and, for me, graduating with honors was gravy. Had I not ditched so many classes in freshman year, I could've been the damn valedictorian!

I turn around in my seat. The auditorium is packed. Mom's wearing her bright pink blouse so I can spot her in the crowd. I see lots of fathers sneaking glances. *Of course.* Mom sees me, smiles, and blows a kiss. Meanwhile, Gabby's making silly faces, crossing her eyes, and pretending to pick her boogers and flick them at me. She makes me laugh and Ross shushes me. I smile and playfully tell him to "fuck off." He doesn't look amused. I hope he didn't take me seriously. But if he did, that's on him ... school's over, loosen up.

The crowd applauds as Principal Bailey steps on stage and takes his place behind the microphone. He's wearing a slick new suit and his tie has pictures of balloons on it. *How festive.* He looks sharp compared to his usual blue polyester suits that are cut way too small and show the outline of his girth below his pants, an extremely disturbing visual. I wonder if someone finally told him. Suddenly, I remember the day in his office when he was drooling over Mom. I swear he got a chubby. *Gross!*

Mrs. Schelding, and her bright red lips, follows behind Bailey, and stands at the table beside him, where a huge flower arrangement of carnations, sprayed with blue and gold paint, sit next to the stack of diplomas. She looks out into the audience and does a curtsey. *A curtsey?* I audit the crowd. Some are smiling, and the rest look confused. *Did she just flashback to a childhood dance recital? Bizarre.*

Bailey adjusts the microphone height, taps on it a couple times, and begins speaking. "Good afternoon, everyone. I'd like to start by welcoming all students, teachers, parents, family, and friends who are joining us today in celebration of Grand Landing High School's Class of 1992." The crowd stands and cheers. "I am honored to be presenting these hard-working and most deserving graduates with their diplomas. These last four years ..."

I turn to Ross and softly say, "blah, blah, get these kids out of my face, blah, blah, you all suck as parents, blah, blah, and blah, thank you." Ross jabs me with his elbow and furrows his brow. *Geez, he has no sense of humor.*

This shit-show can't be over soon enough. Principal Bailey wraps up his speech, and just when I thought we were moving along to receiving our diplomas, I see Valerie walk on stage. Oh goodie, here comes another five-star speech. Valerie Tennor, the Valedictorian, takes her place on stage, pulls out her speech cheat sheet, and away she goes ... in a way-too-chipper tone.

"Hello to all my fellow graduates. It's great to see

your smiling faces. Today is a turning point in all our lives. We will carry on from here to accomplish great things. We will grow older, independent, and more responsible as we move forward in life and ..."

After a few sentences, I block out the rest of it. When everyone stands to applaud, I know she's finished. I join along, not for the glorified future, but my happiness that the damn speech is over. *I wish I had a better attitude about this whole affair.*

At long last, it's time to walk the stage, get our diplomas, shake Principal Bailey's hand, and pause for a picture. I don't want a picture of me in the giant fucking white gown. Especially taken by a photographer standing on the floor in front of the stage. That's the absolute worst angle to shoot from, even anorexic Kate looks fat. I hope she doesn't have a breakdown when she sees the picture. And I'm not being a smart ass, I'm truly hopeful she won't.

As the ceremony pushes forward, and students are called to the stage, the crowd is becoming unruly. Principal Bailey takes a moment to thank the audience for their enthusiasm and politely ask that they hold their applause until all the students have received their diplomas. Apparently, no one heard him. Almost every student called to the stage has a small village in the audience shouting out cheers and clapping. It's over-the-top distasteful and makes me hate being here even more. I look back at Mom again and shake my head. I'm certain she sees the look of misery on my face because her expression is empathetic.

Finally, my name is called. I side-step my way to the end of the aisle and trip over Bryan's feet as I pass by. Thankfully, I don't fall and make a fool of myself. As I walk to the stage, the auditorium is silent. It's obvious that I don't have my entire extended family here, but as soon as Bailey hands me my diploma, Mom and Gabby stand up and start hooting and hollering, clapping, and stomping their feet as loud as possible. *I love them!* Their energy is addictive and before I know it, people I've never seen before are standing and cheering me on. For the first time during this torturous practice, I'm happy.

Eight more letters of the alphabet to go and the ceremony is over. As usual, I get lost in thought. When I got here, I noticed lots of new cars in the parking lot. Then I saw a bow on one. I thought new cars were only graduation gifts in movies. I get jealous for a minute, but only for a minute. My car gets me where I need to be. And with a baby on the way, money will be tight. *Look at me, thinking all responsibly.* Honestly, I do want some sort of graduation present. Nothing ridiculous like a car, but something to mark the occasion.

Matthew Zeller … and, finally, it's over! Students are supposed to walk back onto the stage and behind the curtain before leaving to find their parents. I walk right over to Mom and Gabby. *What are they gonna do, expel me?*

We hot tail it out of the building before the rest of the crowd. After a few pictures of me holding my diploma in my big-ass white gown, I pull it off, roll it up, and throw it at Gabby. She puts it on and starts twirling around singing "congratulations" to me in the tune of "Happy Birthday" as loud as she can. As she spins, the air catches the gown and opens it up, so it looks like a bell. And with that, she got her new nickname, Ding-a-ling. She accepts it with honor, and I give her my gold graduation sash.

In the parking lot, I see balloons bouncing around in the wind above my car. *Aw, they did get me something.* We walk closer, and I see the "Congrats!" balloons are wrapped around my rear bumper. Mom looks at me and smiles like she's up to something.

"You better untie those balloons before driving to the restaurant, Rose."

"Why? I like them there."

"Well, I don't want them to impair your vision while driving. It could be dangerous."

I don't know why Mom is tripping out about it, it's only two balloons, but I do what she asks and walk around the car to untie them. I see why she's smiling. On the bumper, next to my Jimi Hendrix quote, about when the world will know peace, is a new sticker. It's pink and reads "Have you hugged your child today?" Tears of joy bounce off my shoes. Mom always finds a way of letting me know everything's gonna be okay.

Gabby and I get in my car. I see Mom in the rear-view mirror. She's got her hands clasped together and a smile on her face. I take a deep breath, start the ignition, shift to first, leave the school parking lot, and head to my future.

About the Author

*L*abor Day 1974 – I was born, kicking and screaming, in a hospital charity ward in Norfolk, VA. Diagnosed at an early age with bipolar disorder and anxiety, I became dependent upon the arts as a means of escape, expression, comfort, and healing. By keeping journals and sketchbooks for over thirty years, I learned to channel my emotions by putting pen to paper and paintbrush to canvas ... and saved a ton of money on therapy.

As a writer and visual artist, with no predetermined goal, my career path was somewhat left up to chance and opportunity. I studied art education at Virginia Wesleyan College, but when it became critically clear that teaching wasn't my calling, I became the art director of a commercial photography studio. But once I started writing my first book, the chase for my American dream began ... I had never felt more invigorated.

Inspired by my crooked path, *Not Enough* entertains life through the mind of Rose Moon, the witty and mixed-up high school student who anxiously charts her own course through the most trying and turbulent week of her life.

Author Questionnaire

A **Note from the Editor:** Since you have read *Not Enough*, you might enjoy some excerpts from the response by Ada Brooks to the Hidden Shelf author questionnaire ...

***

Provide a brief description of your book:

Shortly before graduation, high school senior, Rose Riley Moon struggles with unbridled anxiety whilst navigating through the most turbulent and trying week of her life. In an increasingly abusive relationship with her intoxicatingly handsome boyfriend, Devin Miller, Rose becomes pregnant and endures unexpected rejection, violence, and, after a dark secret is brought to light, debilitating pain. Rose leans on her irresponsible and pregnant best friend, Gabby Thomas, for emotional support, self-medication for escape, her co-worker, Penny, to confide in, and (despite a temporary let down) her mother, Randy Moon, for support and unconditional love. The good news is that Rose manages to push forward and graduates with peace of mind ... and a gold sash.

What makes your book different from others in the same genre?

The reader lives in the mind of the main character. And ... I wrote it.

Target audience:

I'm thinking females from the age of 13 and up. But anyone with an open mind ... even men. Not to say that everyone will like the grittiness, crudeness, foul language, and drug use. But they might.

Is this book part of a series?

Yes. The next book, *The Backroom*, continues with Rose's path after high school graduation.

Editor's note: the rest of Ada's answer is classified ... she reveals far too much of the story.

What are the most important goals you hope to achieve from publishing your book?

Success. An ongoing career. Opportunity to improve and continue to write great stories. The means to buy a decent house and vehicle. For me, the little things matter most. I've never longed for a mansion or a private jet ... *but a personal chef would be awesome.* And I am prepared to work my ass off to make it possible!

Name five things you want your readers to know about you?

1) I love dogs
2) I am also a visual artist
3) Family is extremely important
4) I am down to earth with a sense of humor
5) I am open-minded, welcoming to new ideas, thoughts, and suggestions.

Describe your personality:

I am wide-open, honest, in your face, and wear my heart on my sleeve.

Sometimes, I'm a little too honest and that wreaks havoc on my issue with hindsight analysis, over-thinking, and sporadic bouts of self-doubt.

When in good spirits, I'm a smiling, sarcastic, joy of a smart ass.

I love to make people laugh and brighten a stranger's day with humor and kindness. Sometimes I'm a little too nice and it's taken the wrong way. Yes, I want you to have a good day and not cry, but no, I don't want to have your baby.

I can also be kinda mean and a little judgmental. But I keep most of that to myself, except when I'm around people I know won't be offended ... or tell on me.

I'm an optimist on my good days. In limited times of distress, however, I am either a hopeless basket case, a woman on a mission to make things better, or an irritable you-know-what.

I am caring and empathetic to others but can also be hyper-sensitive and get my feelings hurt over

126

something small and unexpected.

I stay true to myself and fight for what I believe in. In return, I appreciate honesty, courtesy, a sense of humor, and common sense! I want to believe we are all inherently good.

I am generous and giving. What's mine is yours ... except for my favorite pens, handbags, dog, and husband.

I am very protective and defensive over the people (and animals) I love. Don't you dare talk about my momma ...

I can be a little too trusting and occasionally open myself up to be hurt or misled. Then again, I am highly intuitive and often know when something bad is going to happen. I always trust my gut, as it has consistently proven to be on point.

My extrovert or introvert tendencies are triggered depending on the scene and if I feel comfortable or not. There are way too many variances to speculate.

I enjoy learning and have just learned that this exercise is harder than I thought it would be.

To reach an ending point here ... according to my husband, I'm frisky, sweet, spontaneous, loveable, perverted, creative, impatient, funny, understanding, smart, and occasionally an angry motorist.

I'm a wee bit complicated. But really, who isn't?

Behind-the-Scenes information about this book (What interesting facts or tidbits can you tell us related to your book, or writing it):

When I first started writing this book over ten years ago, I could think of little else. I just dove in with some ideas, but nothing even close to an outline. I stayed up day and night writing and chain-smoking Marlboro lights while _That '70s Show_ quietly played in the background.

When I started writing Not Enough, I was working at a commercial photography studio 45 minutes from home. As I sat in the daily stop-and-go tunnel traffic, I would make notes leaning against the steering wheel. My boss bought me a tape-recorder to save me from getting into a wreck but no matter how many times I tried, I just couldn't get the words in my brain out of my mouth. Luckily, no injuries resulted from my bad habit.

One other thing ... _Not Enough_ is based on true events in my life. Writing it was tough but also therapeutic.

Spring 2024

The Backroom

By Ada Brooks

"Five weeks after graduation …
my tattered heart could barely beat."

Acknowledgements

My grandmother, Estelle Sherman, at the age of 85, was my first editor for *Not Enough*. In the beginning, I was uneasy with her reading some of the content ... specifically sex. When I expressed this, she responded, "Ada, I have five children. What do you think, it was immaculate conception?" She was my heart. And a very talented writer. She left this world at the age of 97. I thank God for every day I had with her, and I holler out the heavens my endless love and gratitude for her wisdom, support, and contributions that helped shaped my life and my writing.

Mom, mom, mom ... how did you do it? Raising me as a single parent was no picnic—I know that. I was a seriously messed-up kid. But there was never a time that you left my side. You're my biggest building block, believing in me no matter what. With your love, support, encouragement, and devotion, I've come further than I ever thought possible. Thank you for giving me the best parts of you, for never giving up on me, and allowing me to capture your essence through the role of Randy Moon. Your beautiful soul is beyond irreplaceable and will live on, through me, forever.

To my stepdad, Ken Whitley, thank you for letting me carry on about writing, the content, the process, my publisher, and everything else that came to my mind while you listened and genuinely matched your enthusiasm with mine. Thank you for bringing me such joy. I'm blessed to have you in my life.

I give my deepest thanks and appreciation to my amazing aunt, Patricia Sherman, the grammar commander. For your knowledge, experience, effort, and amazing dedication to help me get this book up and running. I will be forever grateful. You helped me dip my toes, then pushed me in ... in true Aunt Pat fashion. Thank you with all of my heart.

I dedicate my endless love and thanks to my unbelievably supportive, encouraging, and patient husband, Wade. Thank you for washing the dishes and vacuuming while I silently stared at my computer screen in deep thought or was on a roll banging away at the keyboard. When I felt overwhelmed and doubted myself, you gave me encouragement and told me it means I'm making progress, and I'll figure it out. Your words of confidence gave me the courage to get back on track and continue moving forward. For this and so much more, thank you!

And to my editor and publisher, Bob Gaines, I extend my warmest thanks for acting not only as my editor, but my coach and cheerleader as well. Your direction and suggestions, comments, critiques, humor, and earnestness helped shape the book, my writing, and myself to be stronger than I ever imagined possible. Thank you for taking a chance on me and giving me the opportunity to strive for and realize my dreams.

Explore the Hidden Shelf